Kit Carson:
Indian Fighter or Indian Killer?

KIT CARSON
Indian Fighter or Indian Killer?

R. C. GORDON-MCCUTCHAN

Editor

UNIVERSITY PRESS OF COLORADO

© 1996 by the University Press of Colorado

Published by the University Press of Colorado
P.O. Box 849
Niwot, Colorado 80544
(303) 530-5337

All rights reserved.
Printed in the United States of America.

The University Press of Colorado is a cooperative publishing enterprise supported, in part, by Adams State College, Colorado State University, Fort Lewis College, Mesa State College, Metropolitan State College of Denver, University of Colorado, University of Northern Colorado, University of Southern Colorado, and Western State College of Colorado.

The paper used in this publication meets the minimum requirements of the American National Standard for Information Sciences — Permanence of Paper for Printed Library Materials. ANSI Z39.48-1984

Library of Congress Cataloging-in-Publication Data

Kit Carson: Indian fighter or Indian killer? / R.C. Gordon-McCutchan, editor.
  p. cm.
  Includes index.
  ISBN 0-87081-393-5
  1. Carson, Kit, 1809–1868 — Relations with Indians. 2. Navajo Indians — Wars. 3. Navajo Indians — Relocation. I. Gordon-McCutchan, R. C.
  F592.C33K58 1996
  978'.02 — dc20   96-22229
                                                                  CIP

10 9 8 7 6 5 4 3 2 1

For Harvey L. Carter.
In the field of Carson scholarship,
truly "he led the way."

Contents

Foreword   ix
by Mark L. Gardner

1. Kit Carson and Dime Novels: The Making of a Legend   1
   Darlis A. Miller

2. "Rope Thrower" and the Navajo   21
   R. C. Gordon-McCutchan

3. The Historiography of the Navajo Roundup   49
   Lawrence C. Kelly

4. Kit and the Indians   73
   Marc S. Simmons

5. An Indian Before Breakfast: Kit Carson Then and Now   91
   Robert M. Utley

Contributors   99

Index   101

Foreword

Kit Carson stares out of a photograph in my office. Looking stiff and uncomfortable in his colonel's uniform, hair unkempt and a definite frown suggesting his demeanor, Kit was not the most photogenic of frontier figures. In fact, he sometimes had to be cajoled into getting his portrait taken. Much more bothersome to Kit than the camera's unforgiving lens, though, was the role of mythic western hero that had been squarely thrust upon him before the age of forty — a distorted image of himself that had quickly taken on a life of its own. Nurturing that image along, of course, was an adoring public with a seemingly endless fascination with the famous frontiersman and his exploits, both real and imagined. To a certain extent, that fascination persists to this day, over 125 years after Carson's death, although the adulation so common in the nineteenth century and for much of the twentieth is conspicuously absent. Indeed, the man frozen in my photo has become an entirely different personage to many Americans. Instead of Kit Carson, the "celebrated mountaineer," he is now Kit Carson, the "pint-size, illiterate Indian-killer."[1]

Born Christopher Houston Carson in 1809, Kit's first encounter with notoriety came when he ran away from a dull apprenticeship with a saddler, David Workman, in Franklin, Missouri, in 1826. Workman placed a notice in the local paper, offering a ludicrous one-cent reward for the return of the boy, described as "small of his age but thick-set, [with] light hair."[2] But Kit probably never saw the now-famous notice, which undoubtedly cost more than the reward offered, for he had joined up with a Santa Fe Trail caravan to see the exotic Far West. For the next three years, he led a transient's life on the plains and mountains, working variously as a teamster, cook, and interpreter, before beginning a long and productive career as a beaver trapper, better known today as a mountain man.

Like hundreds of his cohorts who populated the Rocky Mountains while beaver pelts brought high prices in the 1830s, Kit could have ended up just a simple footnote in the annals of the fur trade. A chance encounter on a Missouri River steamboat in 1842, however, foiled all possibility of that fate. On that boat, Kit met Lieutenant John Charles Frémont, who was on his way upstream to begin his first government-exploring expedition in the West. The two took a liking to one another, forged the beginnings of a lifelong friendship, and Frémont hired Carson as a guide at one hundred dollars a month. When Frémont published his report of this expedition and the one following (1843–1844), which Carson also accompanied, the former beaver trapper emerged from its pages as one of the larger stars in the interesting cast of characters that made up Frémont's parties.[3] The report was priceless publicity, and with the help of a few exciting exploits as a dispatch carrier and guide during the Mexican-American War, the public became as smitten with Kit as was his friend Frémont. Kit even had an elegant Missouri River steamboat named for him in 1848 — a significant indicator of celebrity status.[4]

Soon Kit began to appear in works of fiction, and thus the mythical Carson was born. This Carson, a "paragon of mountaineers," wrote one author in 1848, was "an incarnate devil in [an] Indian fight, and had raised more hair from [the] head[s] of Redskins than any two men in the western country."[5] Because of countless such descriptions in numerous works, whenever anyone met the real Kit for the first time, they were invariably disappointed, at least initially. A correspondent of the *Washington Chronicle* who visited Fort Garland, Colorado, in 1867 was

> as anxious as a school-boy to see America's ideal hunter and Indian fighter. Who has not read some fearless exploit, some hairbreadth escape of Kit Carson! I have pictured him to myself as the equal of *Nimrod* — a man of huge stature and powerful limb, with fierce dark eyes, swarthy complexion, and long, black hair and beard; with a voice like a giant; a powerful nature filled with strong passions and governed by noble impulses.

Instead, the correspondent found a soft-spoken man,

> [f]ive feet six in his stockings, deep-chested and squarely set, with the slightest stoop of the shoulders, feet and hands small, an oval face, very young looking for its fifty-eight years of care; light blue eyes, gentle as a woman's and clear as a boys; the mouth well cut, but with straight lines around the corners and the [ap]pearance of having been made from a harder material than the rest of the face; the nose not remarkable; with thorough Saxon hair falling to his shoulders, and looking a little thin on top and streaked with threads of silver; a moustache of the same light color was the only hair on his face.[6]

Despite such doses of reality, the mythical Carson continued to prevail in the American imagination.

After Kit Carson's death in 1868, he endured as one of the truly great frontier heroes, often being mentioned in the same breath with immortals Daniel Boone and Davy Crockett. A Carson artifact, especially a gun, was the Hope Diamond of most any western museum collection. And there was no shortage of biographies (including one based on Carson's own dictated memoirs, which went through several editions). Even those volumes written by serious scholars in the twentieth century, who vigorously chopped away the myth that had grown up around Carson for so long, found the frontiersman deserving of his pedestal. The premier Carson scholar, the late Dr. Harvey Carter, described his subject in 1968 as "a nice guy who finished first." And a biography of Carson he co-authored with Thelma Guild in 1984 appeared with the title *Kit Carson: A Pattern for Heroes*.[7] Yet by this later date, a dramatic shift in the public's perception of Kit was well under way — not everyone thought of him as a hero anymore.

The shift focused on Kit's treatment of American Indians. To have been a rip-snortin' Indian killer, as Kit was often portrayed in the nineteenth century, was definitely not considered admirable or heroic in the late twentieth. Especially singled out for attack was Carson's role as field commander of the military forces in the campaign against the Navajos in 1863–1864, a campaign that saw most of the tribe displaced to the ill-fated Bosque Redondo reservation. Right or wrong, Kit became the villain of this episode, and many scholars and lay people looked at him as much worse, a fact made dreadfully clear to staff members at the Kit Carson Home in Taos, New Mexico, on more than one occasion. In the summer of 1992, a potential visitor to that historic site was overheard to say, "I will not go into the home of that racist, genocidal killer."[8]

That many Americans would accept Kit's transformation from hero to scoundrel without question is not surprising in today's world of celebrity and political scandals, tell-all books, and spin doctors. Debunking seems to be all the rage and promises to continue. A 1994 telephone survey by Scripps Howard News Service and Ohio University found that seventy-three percent of one thousand individuals questioned believed that Americans have "generally become more cynical about heroes."[9] The irony of all this, of course, is that in endorsing the image of Kit as genocidal killer bad guy, Americans have once again disregarded the real man for a flashy myth.

In an effort to counter this pervasive, negative view of Kit, the Kit Carson Historic Museums organized a scholarly symposium for July 31, 1993, entitled "Kit Carson: Indian Fighter or Indian Killer?" to closely examine the fact and fiction of Carson's dealings with various Indian groups. The event was funded by the New Mexico Endowment for the Humanities, and the papers presented that summer day in Taos by several distinguished historians have been gathered into the present volume.

Fittingly, the symposium itself was controversial. The conference organizer touted it as a salvo in the debate between traditional scholars and the new western historians (also labeled revisionists), an angle that the press gladly played up (the *Santa Fe Reporter* ran the bold headline, "The Second Battle for the West").[10] One of Carson's biggest detractors initially agreed to participate in the symposium but then reneged when he learned that a rival scholar had also agreed to speak. Representatives of the Navajo tribe flatly declined an invitation to provide their perspective on Carson. The lofty *New York Times* saw fit to cover the conference (this was nothing spectacular for Carson — his name first appeared in that paper in 1858), and a slew of opinion pieces appeared in the *Taos News* for months after the event.[11] The titles of these latter reveal the intensity of the feelings the symposium generated: "Seminar on Kit Carson fueled racism, ignored truth," "History reveals the truth; Kit Carson seminar defended," "Ludicrous stance: Kit Carson as a friend to the Indians," "'Revisionist history' serves no one but the revisionists."[12] The book in your hands promises to be no less provocative.

Perhaps the best explanation of the spirit in which the following essays are offered comes from the last published work of Harvey Carter, who was the guest of honor at the Taos symposium and to whom this book, quite rightly, is dedicated. "Our devotion is not to Kit Carson, right or wrong," he wrote. "Our devotion is to truth; ascertainable factual truth, without which history becomes mere opinion or deliberate propaganda."[13] A prominent western historian opined before the conference that Kit would be "very angry" that these efforts were being made to defend him.[14] Yet Kit, it seems, was a stickler for the truth also. Jesse Benton Frémont, illustrious wife of the pathfinder, remembered an incident where Carson had objected to a writer's use of the simple phrase, "there he snared the wily beaver" in a sketch of the frontiersman's life. Kit "did not like to hurt the writer's pride; but said he, 'there's men that will read that, and they'll know every word of that had to come from me or them, and it's not true that I *snared* beaver. Beaver must be caught with *traps*.'"15

Just as Kit Carson knew the difference between a snare and a trap, the authors of this volume know the difference between a myth and a fact. Granted, some are quite shrill in their efforts to set the record straight. But I think the real Kit, the soft-spoken, camera-shy trapper, scout, and soldier, would be pleased with them all.

Mark L. Gardner

Notes

1. Advertising flyer for "Discovery Channel's How the West Was Lost," Time-Life Video, 1995. The full quotation, as it appears in a caption beneath a photo of Carson, reads: "The gun-toting good guy of Hollywood westerns, the real Kit Carson was a pint-size, illiterate Indian-killer whose scorched-earth campaign ensured that the Navajo could briefly run but never hide."
2. Edwin L. Sabin, *Kit Carson Days, 1809–1868: "Adventures in the Path of Empire,"* 2 vols. (1935; reprint ed., Lincoln: University of Nebraska Press, 1995), 1:2.
3. John Charles Frémont, *Report of the Exploring Expedition to the Rocky Mountains in the Year 1842, and to Oregon and North California in the Years 1843–'44,* Senate Document 174, 28th Cong., 2nd sess., 1845 (Serial 461). This report was reprinted many times by commercial publishers. Two examples are Samuel M. Smucker, *The Life of Col. John Charles Fremont, and His Narrative of Explorations and Adventures, in Kansas, Nebraska, Oregon and California* (New York: Miller, Orton & Mulligan, 1856) and *The Daring Adventures of Kit Carson and Fremont, Among Buffaloes, Grizzlies and Indians, Being a Spirited Diary of the Most Difficult and Wonderful Explorations Ever Made, Opening, Through Yawning Chasms and Over Perilous Peaks, The Great Pathway to the Pacific* (New York: Butler Brothers, 1885).
4. Frederick Way, Jr., *Way's Packet Directory, 1848–1983* (Athens: Ohio University Press, 1983), 272. This boat burned in the St. Louis fire of 1849. Another steamboat with the name of *Kit Carson* appeared in 1862.
5. George A. F. Ruxton, *Life in the Far West* (New York: Harper & Brothers, 1855), 193–194. This famous novel of the mountain men appeared serially in *Blackwood's Magazine* in 1848 and was first published in book form in 1849.
6. *Rocky Mountain News,* November 5, 1867.
7. Harvey Lewis Carter, *"Dear Old Kit": The Historical Christopher Carson* (Norman: University of Oklahoma Press, 1968), vii; and Harvey L. Carter and Thelma S. Guild, *Kit Carson: A Pattern for Heroes* (Lincoln: University of Nebraska Press, 1984).
8. As quoted in Josh Kurtz, "The Second Battle for the West," *Santa Fe Reporter,* June 30–July 6, 1993, 11.
9. Thomas Hargrove and Guido H. Stempel III, "Heroism: Something We Used to Believe In," *Rocky Mountain News,* August 10, 1994, 34A. The survey also revealed that the group of Americans most inclined to "disavow heroes" was the Baby Boom generation, or what I now call the Walking Disenchanted.

10. Josh Kurz, "The Second Battle for the West," *Santa Fe Reporter,* 12. This debate has now grown quite tired and will not be elaborated on here. For those who dare explore it, see Richard Bernstein, "Unsettling the Old West," *New York Times Magazine,* March 18, 1990; (various authors), "Western History: Why the Past May Be Changing," *Montana: The Magazine of Western History,* 40 (Summer 1990): 60–76; Larry McMurtry, "How the West Was Won or Lost," *The New Republic,* October 22, 1990, 32–38; William Ecenbarger, "The West: Shooting Holes in the Myth," *Contemporary* section, *Denver Post,* November 10, 1991; Alan Brinkley, "The Western Historians: Don't Fence Them In," *The New York Times Book Review,* September 20, 1992; and Gerald Nash, "Point of View: One Hundred Years of Western History," *Journal of the West,* 32 (January 1993): 3–4.

11. "In Defense of a Hero of the Old West," *New York Times,* August 10, 1993, A12. This article was also published in the *Denver Post,* August 22, 1993.

12. *Taos News,* August 19 and 26, September 2, and October 28, 1993.

13. Harvey Carter, "Introduction," in Marc Simmons and R. C. Gordon-McCutchan, *The Short Truth About Kit Carson and the Indians* (Taos, N.M.: Kit Carson Historic Museums, 1993). This small book made its debut at the Taos symposium.

14. Kurz, "The Second Battle for the West," 12.

15. Jessie Benton Frémont, *The Story of the Guard: A Chronicle of the War* (Boston: Ticknor and Fields, 1863), 31.

Kit Carson:
Indian Fighter or Indian Killer?

CHAPTER 1

Kit Carson and Dime Novels: The Making of a Legend

Darlis A. Miller

"The red marauders had come and gone again, but they had left behind them naught but ruin and death. [Tom and Billy Gardner] saw the mangled bodies of the four teamsters where they had fallen, riddled with Indian bullets, and they also found the remains of Aunt Celia, who had been slain by a blow from a hatchet." But the boys looked in vain for their father and Tom's sweetheart, Flora Barron, taken captive by the Indians. Suddenly, they "heard the sound of a horse approaching at headlong speed. Then under the moonlight they beheld a magnificent coal-black steed bounding toward them ridden by a powerfully built man in the garb of a white trapper. . . . 'Kit Carson! The great scout has come at last!' [exclaimed Tom]. . . . 'Yes!' cried the king of scouts. . . . 'I have come at last, but too late to foil the red demons, it seems. I was ambushed up the river by a dozen reds, but after a sharp fight I gave them the slip and here I am.'"[1]

Thus begins a fast-paced, dime novel adventure story that captivated readers nearly a century ago. Dime novels, in fact, helped to create the Carson legend, depicting the famous scout as one of the world's greatest Indian fighters and killers. A popular literary genre, dime novels flooded the newsstands during and after the Civil War, generating stereotypes of Indians and frontierspeople that influenced the public mind well into the twentieth century. Because dime novels played such an important role in creating popular heroes and villains, it will be helpful to look at their origins and development in assessing their impact on the Carson story.

The original dime novels appeared in 1860, the creation of the New York publishing firm Beadle & Adams, consisting of the brothers Erastus and Irwin Beadle and Robert Adams. *Malaeska; The Indian Wife of the White Hunter,* by Ann S. Stephens, introduced the series in June and set the tone for later publications. In this action-packed story, the hero, William Danforth, shoots down a host of "savage Indians" while rescuing his Indian wife, Malaeska, from their clutches. Combining romance and adventure, *Malaeska* sold at least a half million copies. Even more successful was No. 8 in the series, *Seth Jones; or, The Captives of the Frontier,* written by a young schoolteacher, Edward S. Ellis. The hero of this tale is a young aristocratic easterner disguised as a backwoodsman, who slays a multitude of Indians while rescuing captives from the Mohawks.[2]

There was nothing new about this type of adventure story. What distinguished the Beadle & Adams dime novels was their price, format, and regularity of issue. The introduction of the steam-rotary press in the 1840s lowered the cost of printing, allowing the publishers to reach a mass audience. The pocket-sized booklets, enclosed in colored wrappers and containing about a hundred pages, sold for five or ten cents a copy, with new issues appearing about every two weeks. Stamped on the covers were sensational action scenes designed to help sell the novels.[3]

The Beadle thrillers that followed *Seth Jones* proved enormously popular with the public. Writers churned out these adventure stories with great speed, many of them composing at the rate of a thousand words an hour for twelve hours at a stretch. They wrote according to formula. The western dime novel, for example, often featured a young hero rescuing a beautiful heroine from Indians. Henry Nash Smith has said that fiction produced in this manner "takes on the character of automatic writing."[4] Nevertheless, Civil War soldiers devoured this kind of fiction. The little booklets were sent to their camps "in bales, like firewood,"[5] and sutlers distributed them quickly to avoid a scramble for their possession. They also were among the favorite items that Union and Confederate pickets exchanged during lulls in the fighting. Beadle & Adams's total sales between 1860 and 1865 are said to have reached nearly five million copies.

Dime novels, in fact, appealed to readers from all social classes. Bankers, lawyers, clergymen, and presidents read them, along with shopgirls, farmboys, mechanics, train travelers, and lawbreakers. Beadle's instructions to authors ensured that the stories would be chaste, even though they were filled with scenes of violence and bloodshed: "We prohibit all things offensive to good taste in expression and incident; we prohibit subjects or characters that carry an immoral taint."[6] When rival firms entered the field, however, sensationalism increased, and dime novels became synonymous with blood-and-thunder literature. In response to this new competition, Beadle editor Orville Victor explained: "We had to kill a few more Indians than we used to; we held our own against them."[7]

The popularity of dime novels is not difficult to explain. These action-packed melodramas offered mental relaxation from the anxieties and boredom of everyday life. Filled with scenes of romance and adventure, dime novels affirmed values held by ordinary readers: optimism, self-reliance, hard work, courage, and ambition — values seemingly threatened by a rapidly industrializing society. In a nation undergoing phenomenal change, Americans longed for the simpler times that they attributed to their frontier past. Dime novel writers, in fact, glorified western expansion. They depicted the West as a land of opportunity, regeneration, and freedom. Dime novel heroes were agents of civilization, pushing back the wilderness. And in dramatizing the hardships and daily lives of American pioneers, authors boosted national pride and further strengthened their readers' ideals.[8]

When authors wrote about real people, like Kit Carson, Wild Bill Hickok, Buffalo Bill Cody, Daniel Boone, and Davy Crockett, their stories gained the appearance of authenticity, even though the plots bore little resemblance to reality. By projecting onto their fictionalized, historical characters the qualities that Americans most admired, such as courage and self-reliance, writers helped to establish these and other frontierspeople as public heroes.[9]

Nevertheless, despite the moralistic tone of many dime novels, the genre increasingly came under attack as its sensational content escalated. Clergymen, teachers, and moralists condemned the violence and bloodshed featured in nearly every story. Frank Tousey, who began publishing dime novels in 1878, added to the controversy with his stories about Jesse James and other outlaws. In 1883 the postmaster general banned sixty-six issues of Tousey's *Wide Awake Library*, fearing they would incite murder. The following year, the *New York Tribune* claimed that the thrillers had led scores of boys to rob their parents before heading into the wild and woolly West.[10]

Captain Jack Crawford, a nineteenth-century western scout, poet, and lecturer, became one of the nation's most outspoken opponents of dime novels, attacking them relentlessly in his writings and public lectures. He blamed the genre for leading many young men into a life of crime, poverty, and dissipation. The stories, he believed, were responsible for some of the tragedies he had witnessed during the Black Hills gold rush — youngsters lured west by adventure stories only to die from exposure or in brushes with the Sioux. In an essay appearing in his second book of poetry, published in 1886, he wrote: "If I had the power I would catch every dime-novel publisher in America and confine him in prison for life, where he could not pursue his criminal work — for it is criminal — and lead so many bright boys to ruin and disgrace."[11]

Crawford was dedicated to presenting the authentic West to his audiences; hence we can safely assume that if he had read the published reports of John Charles Frémont's first two expeditions west, which first propelled Kit Carson into the public spotlight, he would have applauded them for their faithful portrayal of the western scene. These real-life narratives made Carson a national celebrity a decade or more before Beadle's dime novels were launched.

As an officer in the U.S. Corps of Topographical Engineers, Frémont employed the thirty-two-year-old Carson as guide and hunter on his 1842 excursion to the Rocky Mountains and again on his 1843–1844 trip to Oregon and California. Frémont's reports of his journeys, written in collaboration with his wife, Jessie, fed the public's voracious appetite for information about the West. Congress soon ordered twenty thousand copies of the combined reports, which publishing firms reprinted for the next ten years. They remained best-sellers at least until the outbreak of the Civil War, inspiring an unknown number of adventurous souls to head west.[12]

The Frémont reports are filled with scenes that delight the senses and kindle the imagination. Although submitted as scientific documents, they dramatized the West and created a romantic image of Frémont's small band of explorers. Written with remarkable grace and occasional humor, the reports are exciting to read even today. Kit Carson, for example, quickly captures the reader's imagination as Frémont describes the party's first Indian scare upon entering the range of the Pawnees. Here is his description of Carson investigating a shouted alarm that a large Indian war party was close at hand: "Mounted on a fine horse, without a saddle, and scouring bareheaded over the prairies, Kit was one of the finest pictures of a horseman I have ever seen. A short time enabled him to discover that the Indian war party . . . consisted of six elk, who had been gazing curiously at our caravan as it passed by, and were now scampering off at full speed."[13]

And what reader would fail to experience a vicarious thrill when reading of Frémont's encounters with the vast herds of buffalo blanketing the prairie? On one occasion, Frémont, Carson, and Lucien Maxwell gave chase to a herd numbering between seven hundred and eight hundred. When the beasts became alarmed at their approach, Frémont recalled:

> We started together at a hard gallop, riding steadily abreast of each other, and here the interest of the chase became so engrossingly intense, that we were sensible to nothing else.... [In a few moments] we were going over the ground like a hurricane.... With his eyes flashing, and the foam flying from his mouth, [my horse] sprang on after the cow like a tiger. In a few moments he brought me alongside of her, and, rising in the stirrups, I fired at the distance of a yard.... She fell headlong at the report of the gun, and, checking my horse, I looked around for my companions. At a little distance, Kit was on the ground, engaged in tying his horse to the horns of a cow which he was preparing to cut up.[14]

Calling him "my true and reliable friend," Frémont depicts Carson as a bold frontiersman, an attractive and heroic figure, free of society's constraints. A skilled horseman, expert hunter, and first-rate guide, Carson is fearless in the face of danger, capable of withstanding extreme physical hardships and of overcoming tremendous odds to avenge wrongs committed by "brutal savages." Always reliable and trustworthy, Carson is also modest and unassuming.[15] Such traits were greatly admired by nineteenth-century readers.

These same characteristics, plus Carson's sudden rise to fame, made him an attractive subject for other antebellum writers. Before the Civil War, Carson appeared in a handful of fictional accounts, precursors of the dime novel adventure stories. The first fanciful treatment of Carson, entitled "An Adventure of Kit Carson: A Tale of the Sacramento," was published in *Holden's Dollar Magazine* of New York in April 1848. Two novels followed in 1849: Charles Averill's *Kit Carson, Prince of the Goldhunters* and Emerson Bennett's *The Prairie Flower*. These authors cast Carson as a courageous western hero who rescued beautiful maidens and slayed barbarous Indians. The first Carson biographies also appeared prior to the Civil War. In 1858, DeWitt C. Peters published *The Life and Adventures of Kit Carson, the Nestor of the Rocky Mountains,* based on Carson's dictated memoirs. This was followed two years later by Charles Burdett's *Kit Carson: The Life and Adventures of*

Christopher Carson, The Celebrated Rocky Mountain Hunter, Trapper, and Guide, a retelling of the Peters biography but with more embellishments.[16]

Dime novelists soon exploited Carson's growing fame. The first Beadle booklet featuring Carson as the hero was Edward S. Ellis's *The Life and Times of Christopher Carson: the Rocky Mountain Scout and Guide,* published in 1861.[17] In this and a second novel, published in 1870, in which he used the pseudonym Lieutenant J. H. Randolph, Ellis relied both upon the Peters biography and the Frémont reports to give his stories an aura of authenticity. Ellis had written his first Beadle novel, *Seth Jones,* while teaching school in New Jersey. He continued teaching until the mid-l880s, after which he devoted all his time to writing. Although he was a prolific writer, Ellis wrote under so many pseudonyms that the exact number of his books is impossible to establish.[18]

Nor is it possible to determine the exact number of Kit Carson dime novels that were published or even to identify with certainty their authors. The dime novel scholar Daryl Jones claims that between 1860 and 1900, Carson appeared in more than seventy original stories and reprints.[19] The authors of some of these tales, like Ellis and Julius Warren ("Leon") Lewis, were among the most versatile and successful of the dime novel writers. Lewis started writing at age eighteen and, in collaboration with his wife, Harriet — who possibly was co-author of Lewis's *Red Knife; or, Kit Carson's Last Trail* — became extremely prosperous. The fate of Thomas C. Harbaugh, creator of *Kiowa Charley, The White Mustanger; or, Rocky Mountain Kit's Last Scalp Hunt,* probably was more typical of the sensational novelists. After making a modest living by writing dime novels, short stories, juvenile tales, poetry, and journal articles, Harbaugh fell on hard times and died in an Ohio county poor house.[20]

In more recent times, two cultural historians have explored nineteenth-century writers' portrayal of Kit Carson as a literary character. Henry Nash Smith and Kent Steckmesser both examine the contrasting images found in biographical and fictional accounts. They find that biographers generally depicted Carson as a refined hero, sanitizing his speech and manners so that he became a suitable hero for genteel readers. Dime novelists, on the other hand, usually portrayed Carson as a blood-and-thunder Indian killer, scalping Indians and speaking a tortured western dialect.[21] Building on the Smith and Steckmesser studies, I now explore the Kit Carson dime novels in greater detail, focusing on the images found therein of frontiersmen and women, whites and Indians, as preparation for assessing the continuing impact these stories have had on the public mind.

Like most other sensational westerns, the Kit Carson dime novels describe a masculine frontier, a male fantasy world where Kit survives a series of adventures by outwitting, out fighting, and eventually conquering both white and Indian villains while at the same time rescuing weaker souls, both male and female, from certain death or unspeakable outrages. Carson is repeatedly cast as the frontier's greatest guide, hunter, trapper, and Indian fighter. An expert with the knife, an excellent shot and rider, Carson is unsurpassed in his knowledge of wilderness living. Moreover, he is a brave, noble, honest, and unassuming companion, "valiant in battle [and] gentle in camp."[22]

Much of the novels' action centers on physical combat. Ellis's pseudo-biographical Beadle publications portray Carson as the nation's best Indian fighter, "a perfect devil incarnate in an Indian fight."[23] He is described as "the man who alone had vanquished whole parties of bloodthirsty Indians."[24] In hand-to-hand combat with "a tall, hideous-looking Apache," Carson plunges "his knife to the hilt in the breast of the red-skin, who with a gasp and a groan gave up the ghost."[25] In another fight with Apaches, Carson rages "like a lion among his prey. The ground was plentifully sprinkled with the blood of the savages."[26] Dime novelist Albert W. Aiken writes of a youthful Carson in *Kit Carson, King of Guides.* In this booklet intended for young boys, Kit defeats the "blood-thirsty" Mangas Colorado, "the best fighting man in the Apache tribe," in a pistol and knife duel. Thereafter, "the Apaches looked upon Kit Carson as being something more than mortal." Kit's prowess in battle similarly awes the Comanches, who regard the young scout as "the greatest fighting-man that they had ever encountered."[27]

Carson vanquishes his savage opponents as often by outwitting them as by besting them in physical contests, however. In *Kit Carson, The King of the Scouts,* Kit hits upon a gory technique for frightening his enemies into flight. While attempting to spy on a council of warriors, he nearly decapitates a sentinel who stumbles onto his hiding place. Kit then drags the body of the dead Indian to the base of a tree, places it in a sitting posture with its knees drawn up, and then, "severing the head from the neck," places it in the dead Indian's "hands on his knees." Kit kills a second sentinel on the opposite side of the camp and leaves the headless body in a similar position. When the surviving Indians discover that "another one of their number was holding his head in his hands instead of on his shoulders . . . yells and howls filled the air, and the superstitious sons of the forest fled as fast as their feet could carry them." Carson and his comrades repeat this bloody maneuver at least a dozen times in their next encounter with Indians. This is the type of sensationalism that critics of dime novels deplored. The author does attempt to retain some heroic features for the Kit Carson figure, however, by having him proclaim: "I never murder. I only kill in fair fight."[28]

Indian-white conflict is crucial to the dime novel adventure story. Robert F. Berkhofer writes in *The White Man's Indian* that the western "must be set at the moment when social order and anarchy meet, when civilization encounters savagery, on the frontier of White expansion, in order to give rise to the conflict that is the heart of the genre."[29] Dime novel westerns, then, many of them written while Indian wars still raged in the West, constitute a conquest literature, justifying white subjugation of Native Americans and their land. The savagery of Indians repeatedly is juxtaposed with the heroic qualities of Kit Carson and other white paragons. By depicting Indians as barbarous fiends, or at least as more barbaric than whites, writers of cheap westerns legitimized white society's desire to conquer or eliminate a supposedly lower class of humanity. According to this rationalization, because Indians are savages, they deserve to be killed.

These ideas are expressed, for example, in Edward S. Ellis's *The Life and Times of Christopher Carson,* where the author depicts the Apaches as waging "cruel, unrelenting war." Led by their "notorious chief Chico Velasques, [the tribe] was committing all manner of barbarities. The name of this savage was a terror and execration, for many years, through the adjoining country. It is related that his dress was profusely ornamented with the finger-bones of the victims of his cruelty, while scalps literally covered his wigwam walls."[30] And consider another gory scene in Ellis's *The Fighting Trapper; or, Kit Carson to the Rescue.* The hero of this tale is George Summerfield, a noble-hearted easterner. Held captive by savage Indians, he had listened to their "wild, frenzied shouts and shrieks" as they burned another prisoner at the stake. Summerfield soon visits the site where the "wretch had been burned. Here he saw a sight that made him shudder. [The victim] had been bound to a small tree, and a huge pile of fagots placed around him. These had been fired and had burned nearly every particle of flesh from his body. Below the knees, the bones were white and glistening, without a particle of flesh, while in different parts of the body were clinging a few crisped cinders! The ashes still contained live coals, and the smell of burning flesh filled the air."[31] In these and other Kit Carson westerns, Indians are described as "red demons," "treacherous rascals," "hideous war-painted savages," "red marauders," "cunning and crafty redskins," "red fiends," "hideous in warpaint," emitting "savage yells," "screaming like wild beasts," and dancing around the torture stake "like a band of fiends."[32]

Even though Indians are vital to the novels, they serve primarily as a backdrop for white protagonists. The action swirls around Carson and his compatriots. The Native Americans rarely appear on center stage, because to turn them into more fully realized characters would grant them equal humanity with whites. Even when the scene shifts to an Indian village, white men continue to dominate the action, often appearing as white renegades or as noble white men disguised or living as Indians. In either role, the white man always shows his superiority to the Indian. Nastier than the most barbaric savage, the white outcast dominates his Indian companions, while the noble white man in disguise performs feats only slightly less heroic than those of Kit Carson.

While cheap adventure stories contributed enormously to the public's misinformed vision of Indian life, they also reinforced traditional views of male and female roles in Euro-American society. Like Native Americans, white women are essential to the dime novel western. Yet in this masculine success story of adventure, individualism, action, and violence, women generally play passive roles, either as love objects or as weaker souls dependent upon male heroes for their survival. In fact, the chief function of the dime novel woman is to be protected and rescued by male protagonists. She is not totally devoid of strength of character, however. Often she makes a dramatic escape from her Indian captors — although usually "in an agony of fear" and with the aid of a male accomplice.[33] She shows courage in ways appropriate to her sex. She does not complain about her circumstances, for example, and the source of her strength comes from her faith in God and Kit Carson. Her courage is always linked to her beauty. Bessie Lincoln, held captive by the Kiowas, shoots and kills Black Mustang, one of her captors. Yet men admire her beauty as much as they do her courage. Carson calls her "the beauty of the Plains," and the white man living as an Indian avows that her "beauty outshines the dew of the prairies."[34]

Indian women also appear in the Kit Carson dime novels, sometimes acting as barbarously as their brothers, but on occasion they are cast as powerful medicine women in control of the white hero's fate. The pseudo-biography novels treat minority women with special care, undoubtedly to enlist the reader's sympathy for Carson's real-life marriages to Indian and Hispanic women. In one booklet, Edward S. Ellis briefly mentions Carson's affair of the heart with "an affectionate Indian wife" and, after her death, his marriage to "a Spanish lady of much personal beauty, and of great respectability."[35] In a second account, Carson is united with "a noble-hearted Indian woman" and then a "beautiful and estimable Mexican lady."[36]

In his more fanciful treatment of Carson, Albert W. Aiken writes disparagingly of Mexicans, claiming that as a nation they "are renowned for sloth and idleness." Young Kit and two companions arouse the jealously of Mexican men because their women look upon "the blue-eyed, light-haired race" with favorable eyes. In *Kit Carson, King of Guides*, Kit's future wife, Josefa Jaramillo, rescues Kit and two other trappers from a Santa Fe jail, where they are awaiting execution on false charges of murder. But marriage to Josefa comes only after Carson's life again is saved by a woman, a beautiful Comanche named Silver Bell, "the fairest, red or white, that Carson's eyes had ever looked upon." Disowned by her father for helping Carson escape from sure death, Silver Bell joins Kit at Bent's Fort, where he takes her as his bride. Her subsequent death frees Carson to return to Santa Fe and marry the senorita who had come to his rescue "like an angel from the skies."[37] By performing extraordinary feats of valor, these minority women become acceptable marriage partners for the story's hero.

A comparison of two Carson dime novels appearing a quarter century apart — *Kiowa Charley, The White Mustanger; or, Rocky Mountain Kit's Last Scalp Hunt*, by T. C. Harbaugh, published in 1879, and *Kit Carson's Boys; or, With the Great Scout on His Last Trail*, by an Old Scout, published in 1904 — underscores the persistence of these stereotyped images of women, Indians, and villains. It also shows that the Kit Carson figure basically remained unchanged during these years. Although some concerns of contemporary society are incorporated into the 1904 novel, Carson continues to fight Indians and white renegades and to rescue fair maidens and noble-hearted white men.[38] These stories clearly reveal the standard structure of the dime novel western. In each, the hero embarks on a perilous quest that involves a series of chases, captures, rescues, and hairbreadth escapes. When he ultimately triumphs over evil, the story concludes with a happy ending.[39]

In *Kiowa Charley,* a heroic but aging Kit Carson is quickly introduced to the reader:

> Tall and shaped like a Kiowa, [Carson] might have been mistaken for a warrior of that wily nation, but he was not. He was a white man, but the climate of many Indian lands had tanned his face; he was the best trailer, the grandest fighter, the greatest scout that ever crossed the Mississippi. . . . He had ridden into Sioux camps unattended and alone, had ridden out again, but with the scalps of their greatest warriors at his belt. . . . He had faced the snows of the great West for forty years. His hair had turned from black to gray on the war-path; but he still carried the vigor of youth in his limbs, the ardor of his first trail in his heart. A keener eye was not to be found in the Indian lands of America; a deadlier rifle never rested upon a saddle.[40]

Riding with a small band of scalp-hunters, Kit observes some Kiowas driving a government wagon usually occupied by Bessie Lincoln, daughter of Fort Sill's commanding officer. Thus Kit's quest begins — a dangerous journey to overpower Bessie's abductors and return her safely to her family. Kit is accompanied by two other Indian hunters and young Pepito, who is searching for his lost sister. The most notable of Kit's associates is "Old Experiment," the typical "ugly white man" who appears regularly in cheap westerns. Although he is not the story's villain, this figure is an Indian hater who lives by the maxim that "the only good Indian is a dead Indian." The author calls Old Experiment a grotesque individual; Old Experiment calls himself a teacher — "the great Injun eddicator of the West." With his deadly pistols, he teaches Indians the values of civilization — and then collects their scalps.[41] Daryl Jones points out that dime novelists used the ugly white man's "unrestrained violence as a foil against which to define the character" of the hero.[42] In this story, at least, Kit Carson does not kill Indians indiscriminately.

Two other dime western stock figures that appear early in this novel are the white renegade and the noble-hearted white man in disguise. Both reside in the same Kiowa village and exert power over its inhabitants. Quartz Dick, the villain, displays hard, brown fists that look like lumps of quartz — hence, his name. A quarrelsome rascal, he kills wherever he goes by shooting his victims through the right eye. Kiowa Charley, a noble-hearted white man living as a Kiowa, is nearly as brave and as skilled in combat as Kit Carson. Kiowa

Charley also appears disguised as a cyclops, a single-eyed mystery man who rides at night with a herd of wild mustangs. Two stereotyped female figures, both in need of male protection, provide the romantic appeal: Bessie Lincoln, the heroine, and Staria, a passionate Mexican girl.

As the story unfolds, we learn that Staria is in love with Kiowa Charley, who rescued her from the Apaches five years earlier. How Staria and Kiowa Charley came to reside among the Kiowas is a question that remains unanswered. We also learn that in capturing the government wagon, one young Kiowa was shot and killed by Bessie. But on the terrifying ride to the Kiowa village, Bessie, bound hand and foot, falls through a hole in the wagonbed and is left alone on the plains. Kit Carson and Kiowa Charley learn of this improbable event at the same time and race to capture the prize. For some unexplained reason, Charley holds a long-standing grudge against Kit — and tries to kill him as they speed toward the girl.

Meanwhile, Kit's companions are involved in their own adventures. Disgruntled by Pepito's inexperience, Old Experiment sends him into the Kiowa village to claim Staria as his lost sister. But Old Experiment becomes guilt-ridden for having deliberately sent the youngster "into the jaws of death," so he and his partner, disguised as Indians, enter the village to find him. Quartz Dick discovers their true identity, however, and they are seized by the Kiowas. Kit, also disguised as an Indian, comes to their rescue, whereupon Old Experiment unleashes his weapons, shouting: "I'm the great Injun eddicator of the West! . . . I've spent half of my nat'ral life . . . teachin' Injuns . . . that life is one o' the most unsartinist things that ar'!"[43] After leaving the battlefield littered with the bodies of dead Indians, Old Experiment learns that in the commotion, he has shot and apparently killed his friend, Kit Carson.

Bessie Lincoln also is experiencing hard times. After being rescued by the hard-riding Carson, she falls into the hands of an evil rancher, who is subsequently trampled to death by the wild mustangs controlled by the cyclopean rider. Kiowa Charley then takes Bessie to the Kiowa village, where, in a fit of jealous rage, Staria stabs Bessie, intending to kill her. Meanwhile, to atone for the fatal shot that killed Kit, Old Experiment returns to the village, seeking his own death while "educating" more Indians and building Kit Carson a "monument of Kiowa bones."[44] Eventually, all the good characters are reunited in the village, and the happy ending unfolds. Bessie and Kit, although wounded, are both alive. Kiowa Charley kills Quartz Dick in a knife fight. Pepito and Staria discover that they are not siblings after all, and they fall in love. All ride to Fort Sill, where Bessie is reunited with her father and Staria weds Pepito. Kit Carson, who vows he has ridden on his last scalp hunt, soon dies. Thereafter, Bessie marries the dashing Charles Montgomery, also known as Kiowa Charley.

Action is never lacking in this convoluted adventure story. The same is true of the equally complicated *Kit Carson's Boys,* published twenty-five years later. In fact, few significant changes occurred in the Kit Carson dime novel during those years. Kit is still the king of scouts and the most noble of the plainsmen. Readers are told that "All men admire a brave spirit, but when such a one is not only valiant in battle, but gentle in camp, he is doubly admired. Such a man was Kit Carson, the king of backwoodsmen — a kind of western Bayard, 'without fear and without reproach.' He had naturally acquired great influence over his fellow bordermen, and his name was known and feared by every Indian tribe from the Mississippi to the Pacific coast."[45]

Two white renegades appear in this story, Neal Krumage, a black-hearted clerk, and Dan Gollard, a thieving gunrunner living among the Sioux. Tall Horse, the noble-hearted white man disguised as Indian, provides most of the mystery. Romance focuses on Flora Barron, the sweetheart of the young tenderfoot, Tom Gardner. The main scenes of conflict pit Kit Carson and his companions against a "dangerous, roving band of outlaw savages" led by the white villain, Dan Gollard.

In this 1904 story, however, social tensions found in modern society help to shape the plot, although these elements are far less obtrusive than they are in the popular outlaw and detective dime novels that appeared in the late nineteenth and early twentieth centuries. Some scholars believe that dime novels written after about 1875 serve as social commentary on American society. Written during an "age of increasing class strife and labor unrest,"[46] the villains of these stories are often wealthy capitalists and conniving bankers and lawyers who prey on noble-hearted blue-collar workers. According to Richard Slotkin, in *Gunfighter Nation,* writers depicted the two most popular dime novel outlaws, Deadwood Dick and Jessie James, as "social bandits whose outlawry was a response to injustices perpetrated by corrupt officials acting at the behest of powerful moneyed interests."[47]

Although *Kit Carson's Boys* provides little or no meaningful social commentary, the tale begins in St. Louis, where the evil clerk, Neal Krumage, reveals to a rival firm the financial secrets of his employers, thus destroying the family fortunes of Gordon Barron and Ellis Gardner. These few references to high finance are the only concessions that the author makes to the modern scene; the rest of the story is a typical dime novel western melodrama. Gordon Barron soon dies, having placed the care of his lovely daughter Flora in the hands of Ellis Gardner. The surviving partner then sets out with Flora and his two sons to establish a new life on the western plains. Kit Carson, an old family friend, promises to guide them to their new home. As noted earlier, Indians attack the small Gardner party before Carson makes his appearance, and Mr. Gardner and Flora are carried into captivity. When Kit finally meets up with the two boys, he informally adopts them, and they begin their quest to rescue Flora and her guardian.

It is not necessary to summarize all the subplots in this convoluted story. Suffice it to say that within the span of four pages, Kit falls into a second deadly ambush; the mysterious Tall Horse rescues Carson from the torture stake; a thrilling chase ensues; Kit and the boys rescue a government agent, disguised as a missionary, from the Indians; the young men coolly survive their first deadly combat with "savages"; and Tall Horse temporarily frees Flora from her captors.

As the story unfolds, we learn that the villain, Dan Gollard, and his renegade band of Sioux attacked and looted wagon trains returning from the California gold fields several months earlier. Gollard then stashed his ill-gotten golden booty in a secret cave located in a mountain stronghold. The final drama takes place in this region, where Krumage has joined forces with Gollard. Kit Carson, with the aid of Tall Horse, eventually rescues Flora, Mr. Gardner, and the two boys, also taken captive by Indians. The reader now discovers that Tall Horse is really "Yellowstone Norman," a great scout and Indian fighter, whose brother had been robbed and killed by Gollard and his savage crew. In their final escape from the stronghold, Kit kills Krumage and Yellowstone Norman kills Gollard. The story concludes happily, with the Gardners finally reaching their new western home. Here the boys prosper and eventually become quite wealthy. Predictably, Tom marries the lovely Flora.

The message of both stories is simple: goodness prevails over evil. The heroes vanquish the villains; heroines wed the noble-hearted white men; and righteous, hard-working Americans find success, love, and happiness in the golden West, a land of freedom and limitless opportunity. Through it all, Carson's fame shines like the noonday sun.

Kit Carson was still living when the first fictional accounts of his life hit the newsstands, and the circumstances surrounding his discovery of one of these volumes in an Indian camp in 1849 filled him with remorse. Carson had joined a company of dragoons attempting to rescue Mrs. James M. White from Apaches. Closing in on the Indians, the commanding officer ignored Carson's advice to rush their encampment; in the ensuing delay, the Apaches killed Mrs. White. Carson tells of this event in his dictated memoirs: "We found a book in the camp, the first of the kind I had ever seen, in which I was represented as a great hero, slaying Indians by the hundred. I have often thought that Mrs. White must have read it, and knowing that I lived nearby, must have prayed for my appearance in order that she might be saved."[48]

Carson probably was genuinely embarrassed by the treatment he received in these sensational stories. Colonel Henry Inman, in *The Old Santa Fe Trail*, recorded a second Carson encounter with this lurid fiction, although Inman's story may be apocryphal. In 1866, Inman showed Carson the cover of a story that depicted Kit embracing a woman and the bodies of half a dozen dead Indians at his feet. After studying the illustration, Kit purportedly remarked, "Gentlemen, that thar may be true, but I hain't got no recollection of it."[49]

At the time of his death in 1868, Carson's status as a national celebrity rested, in part, on an image created by sensational writers, and Kit's friends labored to keep his heroic reputation alive and untarnished. Jessie Benton Frémont and Edward F. Beale, for example, both sought to discredit a distasteful image of Carson that California poet Joaquin Miller created in "Kit Carson's Ride," which appeared in an 1871 issue of *Harper's Weekly*. The editors of Jessie Frémont's letters succinctly summarize the controversy: "In his poem Miller had described a fictional ride in which Carson stole a beautiful Comanche girl from her people and then abandoned her when her weaker horse gave out as a raging prairie fire threatened to overtake them. The implication was that Carson's instinct for self-preservation overcame his sense of love and duty."[50] Within days of reading this poem, Jessie Frémont wrote to William T. Sherman, then commanding general of the U.S. Army, asking him to lend his voice in protesting this slanderous attack on their friend's memory. "All we can do to prove our love for our friend," she added, "is to keep his name as he kept it clean and honored."[51]

Beale, whose friendship with Carson dated from the Mexican War, took the most vigorous action in refuting Miller's poem. He first wrote a lengthy criticism of Miller's work, which was published in a Pennsylvania newspaper. Then he composed and published a laudatory poem about Carson, entitled "Kit Carson's Shade." Following Beale's two publications, so many other critics spoke out against Miller's poem that the poet revised its ending; the revision depicts Carson risking his own life to save the Indian girl.[52]

The fact that Miller bowed to public criticism suggests, in part, the power of popular imagery. But the question of Carson's reputation, both then and now, is deeply enmeshed in the complex issue of historical reality. Separating the historic Carson from the legendary Carson requires great skill. His most recent biographers, Thelma S. Guild and Harvey L. Carter, have long held the belief that Kit Carson is one of the nation's most deserving heroes and that much of the Carson legend as conveyed in popular literature is "solidly based upon fact."[53] Now, nearly a decade after publication of Carter's co-authored biography, other scholars, including those in this volume, are taking a new, historical look at Carson's career.

Dime novels played an enormous role in shaping public perceptions of Kit Carson. For several generations of readers, Carson was a national hero, an agent of manifest destiny who helped to tame the savage West. Americans everywhere applauded his heroic deeds and qualities. Yet, in ways not envisioned by nineteenth-century moralists, the Kit Carson adventure stories had a baneful influence on the reading public. Insidiously, the tales perpetuated falsehoods about the West and its inhabitants. Kit Carson became a cardboard figure, with flaws in his character remaining unrecorded. Reiterated countless times, dime novel images took on the patina of truth, and stereotypes became accepted fact. In the same way, dime novelists distorted the life stories of other nineteenth-century western figures. In all these fictionalized accounts, legendary heroes like Wild Bill Hickok, Buffalo Bill Cody, George Armstrong Custer, and Kit Carson — as well as Indians, women, and other minorities — were denied their true humanity.

Indeed, dime novelists helped to create the mythic West. They romanticized white expansion and ignored its destructive elements; they exaggerated the triumphs of white settlers and minimized their failures; they eschewed moral issues regarding Indian-white contact. Their stories simply did not give a true picture of the West. Today, the average college freshman is unlikely to know anything about the historic Kit Carson. Those who recognize his name simply associate it with the mythic West of cowboys and Indians.[54] Even though the dime novel images of Carson as scalp-hunter and Indian slayer may not be foremost in people's thoughts today, Kit Carson novels contributed to the romanticized Euro-American image of Western history that still dominates the public mind. In this way, the dime novel Kit Carson continues to influence the way we think about our western heritage.

NOTES

1. An Old Scout, *Kit Carson's Boys, or, With the Great Scout on His Last Trail* (Pluck and Luck No. 340, New York: Frank Tousey, 1904), p. 5.
2. For discussions of these two novels, see the following sources: Albert Johannsen, *The House of Beadle and Adams and Its Dime and Nickel Novels,* vol. 1 (Norman: University of Oklahoma Press, 1950), pp. 30–33; Emory Elliott, ed., *The Columbia History of the American Novel* (New York: Columbia University Press, 1991), pp. 295–296.
3. For descriptions of the Beadle & Adams dime novels, see Johannsen, *House of Beadle and Adams,* pp. 4, 5, 8. For information on the steam-rotary press, see Daryl Jones, *The Dime Novel Western* (Bowling Green, Ohio: Bowling Green State University Popular Press, 1978), p. 5.
4. Henry Nash Smith, *Virgin Land: The American West as Symbol and Myth* (New York: Random House, 1950), p. 100.
5. Edmund Pearson, *Dime Novels; or, Following an Old Trail in Popular Literature* (reprint, Port Washington, N. Y.: Kennikat Press, 1968), p. 49.
6. Johannsen, *House of Beadle and Adams,* pp. 4, 9.
7. Pearson, *Dime Novels,* p. 99.
8. For discussions of the dime novel's reception, see Ibid., p. 45; Johannsen, *House of Beadle and Adams,* p. 4; Jones, *Dime Novel Western,* pp. 11–26.
9. For discussions of qualities that these fictionalized historical figures personified, see Jones, *Dime Novel Western,* pp. 19, 22, 137, 154–155; Kent L. Steckmesser, *The Western Hero in History and Legend* (Norman: University of Oklahoma Press, 1965), p. 255.
10. The following sources examine the use of violence in dime novels: Daryl E. Jones, "Blood 'N Thunder: Virgins, Villains, and Violence in the Dime Novel Western," *Journal of Popular Culture,* 4 (Fall 1970): 507; Pearson, *Dime Novels,* pp. 92, 223; Dixon Wecter, *The Hero in America: A Chronicle of Hero-Worship* (Ann Arbor: University of Michigan Press, 1963), p. 345; Christine Bold, *Selling the Wild West: Popular Western Fiction, 1860 to 1960* (Bloomington: Indiana University Press, 1987), p. 6.
11. John W. Crawford, *The Poet Scout: A Book of Song and Story* (New York: Funk and Wagnalls, 1886), pp. 15–16.
12. For discussions of Frémont's reports, see Pamela Herr, *Jessie Benton Fremont: A Biography* (New York: Franklin Watts, 1987), pp. 78–83, 110–113; Harvey Lewis Carter, *'Dear Old Kit': The Historical Christopher Carson* (Norman: University of Oklahoma Press, 1968), p. 6.

13. Captain J. C. Frémont, *Report of the Exploring Expedition to the Rocky Mountains in the Year 1842, and to Oregon and North California in the Years 1843–44* (Washington: Gales and Seaton, 1845), p. 15.
14. Ibid., pp. 19–20.
15. Ibid., see especially pp. 119, 237, 261–265.
16. For discussions of the fictional Carson accounts, see Steckmesser, *Western Hero*, pp. 35–37; DeWitt C. Peters, *The Life and Adventures of Kit Carson, the Nestor of the Rocky Mountains* (New York: W.R.C. Clark, 1858); Charles Burdett, *Kit Carson: The Life and Adventures of Christopher Carson, The Celebrated Rocky Mountain Hunter, Trapper, and Guide* (Philadelphia: G. G. Evans, 1860.)
17. See Edward S. Ellis, *The Life and Times of Christopher Carson: The Rocky Mountain Scout and Guide* (New York: Beadle, 1861).
18. For the Ellis novel published in 1870, see Lt. J. H. Randolph, *Carson, the Guide; or, Perils of the Frontier* (New York: Beadle & Adams, 1870). For discussions of Ellis's novel, see Steckmesser, *Western Hero*, p. 39; Johannsen, *House of Beadle and Adams*, vol. 2, pp. 93–94.
19. Jones, *Dime Novel Western*, p. 58. See also J. Edward Leithead, "Buckskin Men of Forest and Plain," parts 1–2, *Dime Novel Round-Up*, 21 (March, May 1953): 18–22, 34–37.
20. For information on Lewis and Harbaugh, see Johannsen, *House of Beadle and Adams*, vol. 2, pp. 128–130, 183–186.
21. Henry Nash Smith, "Kit Carson in Books," *Southwest Review*, 28 (Winter 1943): pp. 174–187; Steckmesser, *Western Hero*, pp. 24–45.
22. Old Scout, *Kit Carson's Boys*, p. 4.
23. Randolph, *Carson, the Guide*, p. 11.
24. Ellis, *Life and Times of Christopher Carson*, p. 36.
25. Randolph, *Carson, the Guide*, p. 3.
26. Ellis, *Life and Times of Christopher Carson*, p. 92.
27. Albert W. Aiken, *Kit Carson, King of Guides; or, Mountain Paths and Prairie Trails* (New York: Beadle & Adams, 1882), pp. 4, 6, 14.
28. An Old Scout, *Kit Carson, The King of the Scouts* (Pluck and Luck No. 504, New York: Frank Tousey, 1908), pp. 10–13, 22.
29. Robert F. Berkhofer, *The White Man's Indian: Images of the American Indian From Columbus to the Present* (New York: Random House, 1978), p. 97.
30. Ellis, *Life and Times of Christopher Carson*, p. 79.
31. Edward S. Ellis, *The Fighting Trapper; or, Kit Carson to the Rescue* (New York: Frank Starr and Co., 1874), p. 18.
32. These descriptions are found in the following sources: Old Scout, *Kit Carson*, p. 12; Randolph, *Carson, the Guide*, p. 9; Old Scout, *Kit Carson*, p. 4; Old Scout, *Kit Carson's Boys*, pp. 5, 8, 10, 11, 6; Ellis, *Fighting Trapper*, p. 17; Old Scout, *Kit Carson's Boys*, p. 6.
33. Old Scout, *Kit Carson's Boys*, p. 11.
34. T. C. Harbaugh, *Kiowa Charley, The White Mustanger; or, Rocky Mountain Kit's Last Scalp Hunt* (New York: Beadle & Adams, 1879), pp. 5, 6.
35. Ellis, *Life and Times of Christopher Carson*, pp. 36, 47.
36. Randolph, *Carson, the Guide*, pp. 17–18.
37. Aiken, *Kit Carson, King of Guides*, pp. 6, 8, 13, 11.

38. See Richard Slotkin, *The Fatal Environment: The Myth of the Frontier in the Age of Industrialization, 1800–1890* (New York: Atheneum, 1985), p. 204; Jones, *Dime Novel Western,* pp. 56–61.
39. Discussions of structure in dime novel westerns are found in the following sources: Jones, *Dime Novel Western,* pp. 135, 137–138; Bold, *Selling the Wild West,* pp. 11, 13.
40. Harbaugh, *Kiowa Charley,* p. 2.
41. Harbaugh, *Kiowa Charley,* p. 9.
42. Jones, *Dime Novel Western,* p. 33.
43. Harbaugh, *Kiowa Charley,* p. 9.
44. Ibid., p. 13.
45. Old Scout, *Kit Carson's Boys,* p. 4.
46. Jones, *Dime Novel Western,* p. 155.
47. Richard Slotkin, *Gunfighter Nation: The Myth of the Frontier in Twentieth-Century America* (New York: Atheneum, 1992), pp. 127–128. For a recent look at dime novels as social commentary, see Michael Denning, *Mechanic Accents: Dime Novels and Working-Class Culture in America* (New York: Verso, 1987).
48. Milo Milton Quaife, ed., *Kit Carson's Autobiography* (Lincoln: University of Nebraska Press, 1967), p. 135.
49. Henry Inman, *The Old Santa Fe Trail: The Story of a Great Highway* (New York: Macmillan Co., 1898), p. 381.
50. Pamela Herr and Mary Lee Spence, eds., *The Letters of Jessie Benton Frémont* (Urbana: University of Illinois Press, 1993), pp. 402–403.
51. Ibid.
52. Gerald Thompson, " 'Kit Carson's Ride': E. F. Beale Assails Joaquin Miller's Indecent Poem," *Arizona and the West,* 26 (Summer 1984): 135–152.
53. Thelma S. Guild and Harvey L. Carter, *Kit Carson: A Pattern for Heroes* (Lincoln: University of Nebraska Press, 1984), p. 294.
54. Based on the author's survey of approximately two hundred students enrolled in her three history courses during spring semester of 1993.

CHAPTER 2

"Rope Thrower" and the Navajo

R. C. Gordon-McCutchan

The Navajo called Kit Carson "Rope Thrower," an apt name because he figuratively captured the entire tribe in his lasso. In the nineteenth century, many considered Carson's defeat of the Navajo his greatest victory. Today, many consider that defeat Carson's greatest infamy. Judging books by their covers, two of the primary indictments of Carson for his role in the Navajo campaign are Lynn R. Bailey's *The Long Walk: A History of the Navajo Wars, 1846–1868* and Clifford Trafzer's *The Kit Carson Campaign: The Last Great Navajo War*. The dust jacket of Bailey's book gives us this summary of Carson's campaign:

> Exactly one hundred years ago commenced one of the most pathetic and tragic episodes in the history of Anglo-Indian relations. Under the ruthless direction of General James Carleton and Colonel "Kit" Carson the Navajo Indians of New Mexico were relentlessly pursued, rounded up and driven to a wretched disease-ridden reservation on the banks of the Rio Pecos in east-central New Mexico — the infamous Bosque Redondo.

A *Booklist* review of Trafzer's work, reprinted on the back cover of the paperback edition, summarizes his thesis:

> Trafzer presents in precise, authoritative style the Navajo's side of Carson's notorious campaign against the tribe in the 1860s. To say the least it was a grim affair — years of ruthless destruction of the Navajo people and their property — and author Trafzer accordingly presents a detailed account, backed up both by an enormous amount of archival research and oral history provided to him by the Navajos.

These quotations sum up the attitude of a large cadre of writers who damn Kit Carson for the Navajo War. Because Trafzer's book is recognized as probably the leading academic authority on this conflict, and because it develops, in one form or another, most of the criticisms to be found in other works, I will concentrate my analysis on the theses advanced against Carson by Professor Trafzer. In taking him to task, I will rely for aid upon Lawrence C. Kelly's excellent book, *Navajo Roundup*. His intelligent gloss on the numerous campaign-related dispatches and letters, which he reproduces in *Navajo Roundup,* is a dependable guide to the facts concerning Carson and the Navajo.

Rhetoric and Presentism

A look at the rhetoric in Trafzer's book reveals a great deal about his biases. In his preface, Trafzer mentions Carson along with Davy Crockett, Wyatt Earp, and Billy the Kid as famous figures in the American West and then glosses: "Many of the 'infamous' people of the West had something in common — they were killers. That is not to imply that they were all cold-blooded murderers, but many killed other human beings and became famous for their exploits. Carson was considered a great 'Indian fighter,' which meant that he killed his share of Indians during his days as a trapper and scout."[1]

Despite his disclaimer ("That is not to imply that they were all cold-blooded murderers"), clearly that is just what Trafzer does mean to imply. His rhetoric is an attempt to confuse in the reader's mind the distinction between a soldier and a killer and to identify Kit with "infamous" murderers like Billy the Kid. As Trafzer says later in his book, "Kit was a simple man of 'sound' character (except that he killed people from time to time, particularly Indians."[2] Notice that Trafzer puts "sound" in quotation marks and then makes Carson's killing of Indians an exception to the fact that he was of "sound" character. The implication is clearly that there was something wrong with Carson's killing of Indians, that from "time to time" he just sort of took it into his head to kill a few innocent savages.

And what of the Navajo? To Trafzer they are "valiant raiders,"[3] "mighty raiders,"[4] and "skilled marauders."[5] He carefully avoids presenting the reader with the massive evidence that convicts the Navajo of repeatedly breaking treaties and attacking the Pueblo Indians and settlers. He avoids this evidence because he wants to convince the reader that the Navajo campaign was not a war against a fierce and aggressive people but rather a slaughter of innocents.

This bias comes out clearly in a discussion about the importance of having horses. Trafzer says that having a horse was often the difference between life and death for the Navajo and then comments, "The soldiers needed horses as well, but they were not fighting for their lives."[6] That line would have been a hard sell to the soldiers in Carson's command who suffered numerous raids on their post, attacks upon wagon trains, and death at the hands of Navajo warriors. But it suits Trafzer's purpose because he needs to convince the reader that Carson was not a soldier but a killer and that the Navajo campaign was not a war but a ruthless slaughter of a guiltless, pastoral people.

Trafzer's role reversal is an interesting one. One hundred and twenty-five years ago, the public perceived Indians as barbaric savages who were killing innocent settlers and who got their just desserts at the hands of soldier scouts like Carson. Carson was a hero fighting bloodthirsty savages and making the West safe for "civilization." In Trafzer's eyes, the "savages" are now "valiant marauders" who had been driven to raiding by the white man. They have become innocent victims of government policy, victims who were simply fighting to preserve their homeland and, through dastardly military measures, were done in by bloodthirsty killer Kit Carson. The Indians have become innocent victims and Carson the guilty party. My purpose here will be to examine Trafzer's book to see how he makes this argument run and then to derail it with the historical facts.

Justification for the Navajo War

To condemn Kit Carson for his role in the Navajo War, one must prove either that the Navajo were completely innocent or that Carson did things in the campaign that violated the principles of just warfare. If, indeed, the Navajo were engaged in behavior that warranted military reprisal, then Carson cannot be condemned, because his campaign was one of self-defense. If the campaign was justified, the question then becomes: How did Carson conduct it?

Let us take up these questions in turn. In doing so, I will defend the view that in this clash of cultures Carson was a man of honor — an Indian fighter, not an Indian killer — whose behavior was justified by the aggressions and atrocities of the Indians and who engaged Indian warriors on the field of battle in a struggle for territorial dominance. I maintain that if settlement were going to occur, then something had to be done to eliminate the warlike tendencies of the Navajo. Peaceful agriculturists, ranchers, and mercantilists simply could not coexist with Indians who preyed upon them.

Was the Navajo War justified? I will argue that any fair appraisal of the facts must insist that it was — *if* you accept the legitimacy of anyone else being present in the Americas other than the indigenous people. It is well known that many Indian tribes, including the Navajo, based their culture on warfare and raiding. Their society did not reach the heights of militarism characteristic of plains Indian culture, but it did make social status dependent upon wealth in animals, animals that could be acquired by the younger and poorer members of the tribe only through warfare with and stealing from the New Mexico settlers. Navajo aggressions were born of an assumption at the very heart of their culture: social status is achieved through raiding to acquire wealth. The very nature of Navajo culture made it difficult for young braves to attain social status without raiding and conflict. Although the old men of the tribe may have been for peace, they could not control their younger members, who wanted to achieve wealth and status by raiding. With the removal of the federal troops that contained these impulses (a removal that began in 1861 with the commencement of the Civil War), the young members of the Navajo tribe launched devastating attacks that called for a military solution.

Further justification for Navajo acts of war came from the concept of "the people." The Navajo's very name for themselves, Diné, means "the people." Moral obligations only governed one's behavior toward members of the tribe. Things one could not do to members of the tribe, one could do to those who were not of "the people." It was wrong to steal from, kill, or enslave other members of the tribe, but such behavior was actually encouraged in the case of whites, or Hispanics, or Pueblo, or Ute Indians.

In analyzing the Navajo War, we must remember that it is easy for us to dismiss the Navajo threat because we are not the ones being attacked by a band of hostile, armed, and historically warlike people. Nor do I think it healthy for the Navajo to ignore the facts. The very qualities that they so admire in their forebears — valor, warrior spirit, horsemanship, strength, survival knowledge, and religious convictions — are many of the same qualities that made the Navajo such a threat to peaceful ranchers and agriculturists.

One good thing about the old western film genre was that it made the Indian threat real. Without that very real threat, there could have been no white heroes. Heroism requires a villain, and certainly the Navajo did plenty of things to warrant casting them in villainous roles. My purpose here is not to recount Navajo atrocities. It is only to point out that the atrocities were very real and were justified by the very nature of Navajo culture. There is too little space here to go through the historical record to prove that for decades the Navajo attacked and raided the Pueblo Indians and Hispanics, to prove that the Navajo broke at least six peace treaties from the arrival of Kearny in 1846 to the Canby peace treaty of 1861, or to detail the Indian horror that engulfed the New Mexico settlers with the troop removal at the outset of the Civil War. The record is there for all fair-minded scholars to study. The Indian threat was very real and so was the military response that ended it.

U.S. MILITARY POLICY

U.S. military policy regarding hostile Indian tribes was simple: It was committed to a belief that Indian cultures based upon raiding, theft, and killing simply could not continue. Henceforward, all cultures had to be based upon principles of peaceful, cooperative effort. Whatever ill we may say of the various implementations of this policy — such as broken treaties, executions, and unwarranted forced relocations — we must nonetheless recognize that the basic policy of overall peace rather than incessant warfare was essentially good. It was simply not possible to allow warlike Indian cultures to remain in existence. Too many innocent people were getting killed as a result.

Given nineteenth-century Navajo cultural assumptions and hostile behavior, the war against them, while harsh, appears to have been the only measure that would end forever a culture based on herding and raiding, a culture that had to end if more peaceful people were to be allowed to survive and prosper. Had the Navajo not resumed raiding at the outset of the Civil War, they would in all probability have ended up like the Utes, who were at peace in 1863, who were never removed from their ancestral hunting grounds, and who are still living in their homeland today. As long as the Navajo do not accept their share of the responsibility for the conflict, they nurture hatreds that are difficult to transcend.

THE WAR ITSELF

General E.R.S. Canby thought, perhaps naively, that his campaign against the Navajo in 1860–1861 was going to be the last Navajo war. When he presented his terms of peace to the defeated Navajo headmen on February 15, 1861, he was convinced that past problems with the Diné were over. So confident was he of this assessment that he ordered the abandonment of Fort Defiance. Had not the Civil War broken out soon after the signing of the Navajo treaty, there really might have been peace. Unfortunately, for all concerned, the Civil War created conditions that led the Navajo to recommence their hostile ways.

Most southern sympathizers soon deserted their western army posts and made their way back to Dixie to enlist in the Confederate forces. In addition, many of the best pro-Union army men were called east to fight the Rebels. These events drastically reduced the number of troops available to ensure that the Navajo kept the peace. Further emboldening the Navajo was the mid-1861 attack launched against New Mexico by thirty-five hundred Texas volunteers serving in the Confederate army. Their objective was to march up the Rio Grande valley, capture New Mexico for the South, and cut off the overland routes to California. All of the U.S. troops available were deployed to halt the Confederate advance, and the Navajo quickly realized that they could resume their attacks on the settlements without fear of retaliation. As Bailey says, "Indian depredations greatly increased during the time New Mexico was being torn asunder by civil and military strife occasioned by the Texas invasion. Navajos on the west, Mescalero Apaches to the east, and Comanches and Kiowas ran riot in the south. Raids became so frequent and intense that a great many people were impoverished by livestock losses, and many farms and settlements were abandoned."[7]

The Confederate threat to New Mexico ended in February 1862 with the defeat of the Texas column at Glorieta Pass. The government then turned its attention to halting the Indian attacks and assigned this task to Canby's successor, Brigadier General James H. Carleton, who was appointed military commander of the New Mexico Territory in the fall of 1862 when Canby was ordered to the eastern battlefields.

Carleton succeeded Canby, but not before the latter had laid down the basic strategy to be pursued in the Navajo War: attack the Indians during all seasons and demonstrate that they could no longer commit depredations and flee to their strongholds — force them to surrender and then remove them to a reservation. Canby felt that removal of the Navajo to a remote reservation, away from their traditional enemies, the Pueblo Indians and the Hispanics, was the only way to ensure peace.

Canby understood that the Navajo would never keep the peace as long as they could sign treaties and break them at will, then flee to their mountain strongholds with little fear of consequences. Nor could their safety from the attacks of the Pueblo Indians and Hispanics be guaranteed as long these ancient enemies lived near enough to raid the Navajo. It was also Canby who selected Carson as field commander for the Navajo War, a choice that, as we shall see, greatly pleased Carleton.[8]

The important point to remember is that the Navajo initiated the hostilities that led to the campaign against them. Had they honored the terms of the Canby peace treaty (whose terms were really quite liberal), there would have been no war. Furthermore, we must bear in mind that it is easy for us today to dismiss the Indian threat faced by New Mexico settlers and to see the Navajo as poor helpless victims. The frequency and severity of Navajo attacks, however, compelled the government to take military measures, and to General Carleton fell the task of implementing Canby's solution.

Carleton was very familiar with New Mexico, having served there previously in the military. Equally important was his friendship with Kit Carson. Kit had served as scout for the troops commanded by then-Major Carleton in the war against the Jicarilla Apache in the 1850s. During that campaign, a well-known incident occurred that resulted in the major presenting Carson with a custom-made hat.

Carson and Carleton were trailing a band of hostile Jicarilla whom they had been pursuing for five days. The morning of the sixth day, after carefully reading the Apache tracks, Kit told the major that they would overtake the fleeing band at two o'clock that afternoon. Major Carleton promised that if they did, he would present Kit with "one of the finest hats that could be procured in New York." Just as Kit predicted, the troops surprised and attacked the fugitive band at precisely two o'clock. Making good on his word, Carleton later gave Kit a beautiful hat with an inscription on the band reading, "At two o'clock, Kit Carson from Major Carleton." From that time forward, Carleton and Carson became friends and professional allies, a combination that was to have serious consequences for the Navajo.

Strategically speaking, Carleton and Carson were an ideal pair to implement Canby's strategy because both fully agreed with it. Both felt that the only solution to the Navajo problem was to militarily force the Navajo to surrender and then remove them to a reservation.[9] As early as 1857, Carson filed a report in which he said, "Humanity, as well as our desire to benefit the Indian race, demands that they be removed as far as practicable from the settlements." He believed Indian survival depended upon removing the tribes to reservations away from the morally degrading temptations of white settlements, training the young in agricultural techniques in order to make them self-subsistent, and stationing troops near the Indians "for the purpose of protecting them from hostile tribes, and also to show unto them that the government has the power to cause them to remain on the lands given them, and not to encroach on that of their neighbors."[10] Carson's proposed Indian policy of 1857 became almost exactly that followed by Carleton at the Bosque Redondo beginning in 1864.

On a personal level, however, Carson was a "reluctant warrior."[11] He had volunteered for army service to fight Confederates, not Indians, and he did not want to get involved in the Navajo War. He felt that he had been away from his family too much and was looking forward to spending the remainder of his days in Taos with his wife and children. His friendship for Carleton, however, and a sense of duty to his fellow New Mexicans, finally induced him to accept the position of field commander.

Carleton and Carson's first job was to subdue the Mescalero Apache, which they did in a short campaign lasting barely two weeks. In the fall of 1862, Carson's troops quickly defeated the Mescalero and by spring 1863 had sent the vanquished four hundred survivors to the Bosque Redondo. Carleton and Carson then turned their attention to the much larger problem of subduing the Navajo.

In December 1862, General Carleton informed a delegation of Navajo headmen that if they wanted to avoid war they had to surrender and agree to relocation to the Bosque Redondo. The Indians seemed shocked and made no reply. When Carleton heard no more from them, he began to prepare for war. In early summer he gave the Navajo a final ultimatum: they had until

July 20, 1863, to surrender and immigrate to the Bosque Redondo; "after that day every Navajoe [sic] that is seen will be considered as hostile, and treated accordingly. . . . after that day the door now open will be closed."[12] When the Navajo failed to surrender as requested, Carleton readied his troops for battle.

Just two weeks after the surrender deadline passed, Colonel Carson went out on his first scout of the Navajo War. He was on patrol for most of August 1863. Disturbing news greeted him upon his return to Fort Defiance (renamed Fort Canby by Carleton). While Carson was in the field, he had left Major Thomas Blakeney in command of the depot guard. On August 26, 1863, four Navajo arrived at the fort under a flag of truce and said that they had come to surrender themselves and their band in accordance with Carleton's ultimatum.

Accounts of what then happened differ, but it appears most likely that Blakeney himself ordered the imprisonment of the Navajo and gave orders that they should be set to work policing the camp grounds. The day after their surrender, two of the Navajo were shot and killed. Blakeney claimed that they were shot while trying to escape, while others in the command testified that Blakeney ordered the Indians' execution. Whatever the truth of the matter, the practical consequences were unfortunate indeed. The leaders of a band of Navajo had attempted to surrender their group but ended up getting killed in the process.

As a result of Blakeney's apparent treachery, the Navajo became convinced that Carson's was a war of extermination, not relocation as Carleton had led them to believe. Henceforward, their strategy was simply to melt away when confronted by force and to launch lightning raids at times and on targets of their own choosing. During the next few months, despite several scouts into Navajo country, Carson and his troops rarely encountered, much less killed, enemy warriors. Carson himself felt chagrined that he could report such a paucity of actual military action and was under continual pressure from Carleton to produce more tangible results. As Carter and Guild say, "At no point could the Navajo Campaign be called glamorous or heroic. It was a military operation in which few persons were killed and no real battles fought."[13]

Unable to confront the Navajo in battle, Carson concentrated on eliminating their supply base. His reports to Carleton are filled with accounts of destroying the Navajo grain fields and other food sources. On one scout alone he reported the destruction of two million pounds of grain. Although the other scouts produced less spectacular totals, it seems likely that Carson's troops destroyed at least 3.5 million pounds of foodstuffs. If we divide that total by twelve thousand, the estimated Navajo population at the beginning of the campaign, we find that Carson destroyed more than 290 days worth of food, figuring a pound of grain per day per person.

In addition, because the Navajo were continually pursued by the troops, they found it very difficult to hunt in their accustomed places. Making survival even more precarious was Carson's destruction of Navajo lodges and clothing. When Carson found a Navajo camp, the inhabitants quickly fled, leaving behind all of their possessions. These Carson burned, leaving the Navajo without protection from the harsh winter. Nor could they build fires for warmth, because the smoke and light would give away their position. The net result: by the end of 1863 the Navajo were harried, freezing, and on the brink of starvation.

Faced with death at the hands of the elements, a few Navajo decided to risk surrender. These Carson treated with kindness, providing them with food and clothes. He explained to them Carleton's policy: that the government would feed, care for, and protect them if they would surrender and immigrate to the Bosque Redondo. The destitute Indians had little choice but to trust Carson, because they were faced with certain death through starvation and exposure. Carson sent the captives back to their bands with his message of support and protection, and the Navajo began a massive surrender. Kelly puts it well when he says that Carson's "treatment of those Navajos who surrendered was more than generous, and there is no doubt that his kindly method of dealing with the captives was an important factor in the subsequent wholesale surrenders."[14] By the end of January 1864 the last great Navajo war was over. More than eight thousand Navajo eventually surrendered and made "the Long Walk" to the Bosque Redondo.

Professor Trafzer and Carson

Carson the Bumpkin

Trafzer registers several criticisms of Carson for his conduct of the Navajo War. First, Trafzer characterizes Carson as a sort of simple bumpkin overawed by Carleton and mindlessly deferential to his superior. Trafzer says that Kit "often yielded to casual adulation and could be persuaded and maneuvered through words of praise, flattery, and commendation."[15] Trafzer provides no evidence to support this assertion, which flies in the face of all other accounts of Carson written by his contemporaries.

It is well known that adulation and flattery embarrassed Carson and that he was a rather modest man who never made much of his fame. It is true that Carson was socially self-conscious and somewhat intimidated by polite society, but he was an exceptionally independent-minded individual little given to being maneuvered by anyone. Although Kit did not want to fight the Navajo War, he was not "maneuvered" into doing so — he simply answered the calls of duty to his fellow citizens and friendship with Carleton and reluctantly undertook the responsibility. That Carson had a strong sense of duty is hardly a personality trait to be criticized.

Carson the Tool

Trafzer intensifies his "personality" attack on Carson in saying that "Kit never questioned the wisdom or necessity of the general's orders and policies. In short, Carson was Carleton's tool, and he permitted himself to be used by the general."[16] That characterization is highly suspect. To begin with, Carson questioned his very appointment as field commander, making clear to Carleton that he did not want to fight the Indians. Also important is the fact that once Carson accepted the command, he was bound to obey the orders of his general. If Carson and Carleton at times disagreed, and the evidence is clear that they did, then the general had the final say. But that is not to Carson's discredit — that is simply the nature of military service. Carson was not a mindless tool maneuvered into carrying out Carleton's policies; we have already seen that as early as 1857 Kit himself had gone on record as endorsing the Indian policy later developed by Canby and Carleton for the Navajo. It's hardly fair to say that Kit was a mindless tool maneuvered into carrying out a plan which he himself developed years before it became official policy.

When we look at the records of the campaign, we find several instances of Carson disagreeing with Carleton. Some examples follow.

1. Carleton had ordered Carson to make his base of operations the Pueblo Colorado. After surveying the site, Carson wrote Carleton informing him that it was unsuitable because it lacked forage for the animals, timber for building, and sufficient water. Carson preferred the reestablishment of Fort Defiance and ordered his troops to encamp there to await Carleton's approval for this change in plan.[17] Carleton saw the sense in Carson's reasoning and acceded to Kit's wish to operate from Fort Defiance.

2. Not long after the aforementioned disagreement, Carson had his first encounter with the Navajo, and an account of the skirmish somehow reached Carleton before Carson's official dispatch. Carleton was furious that Carson himself had not already conveyed this information, and he sent Carson a heated letter instructing him: "send me a weekly report in *detail* of the operations of your command."[18] Carson replied,

> General. I have the honor to acknowledge the receipt of your letter of the 7th inst. In answer I would respectfully state that on the 25th ult I forwarded you a report of the operations of my Command by Capt. B. C. Cutler A.A.G. Since I left on this scout I have had no opportunity to post you on my movements, nor will I be able to communicate with you again until my return to Fort Defiance which will be about the 5th of next month. When leaving on a Scout my course is generally governed by circumstances, and owing to the nature of the service, it would weaken my force too much to send to Defiance or elsewhere a weekly express. I would have to send a strong party with each, which could not again join me during the scout. However, I shall take every opportunity to keep you advised of my movements and of my operations in detail.[19]

Does that sound like the report of a man who "never questioned the wisdom or necessity of the general's orders and policies"?

3. In November 1863, Carson planned to make one last long scout and asked Carleton for a leave of two months at its conclusion. Kit thought that his animals needed time to rest and that further campaigns would have to be postponed "until the weather opens [sic] sufficiently to permit of more extended operations."[20] Carleton refused and insisted that Carson remain in the field. Carleton was especially adamant about Kit making a winter foray into Canyon de Chelly. Carson resisted this idea, convinced as he was that "few, if any Navajoes are in the Canon."[21] Although Carson reluctantly obeyed Carleton's orders, the important point is that Carson forthrightly

told the general that he thought his plan a bad one and gave his reasons why — hardly the behavior of a mindless "tool." Of course, Carleton turned out to be right and Carson wrong, but the incident points up Kit's independence and willingness to speak his mind.

4. The final example of Kit's independent thinking concerns the actual surrender of the Navajo. Carleton was of the opinion that the Navajo numbered at most sixty-five hundred members, while Carson and Captain Asa Carey thought that estimate too conservative. Both were of the opinion that the six thousand who had surrendered by March 1864 represented only half of the tribe. Disagreeing with Carleton's estimate, Carson wrote, "There is no doubt in my mind but that the strength of the Navajo Nation has been underrated, and that there is five or six thousand still at large; and these the most wealthy and powerful."[22] Carson then went on to outline the strategy that he thought would force the last of the Navajo to surrender, closing his letter with this optimistic reassurance: "With this, or a similar plan of campaign, I think I could assure the General of the close this Summer, and forever, of the Navajo War."[23] Would a mindless "tool" disagree with his general on so crucial a matter as the remaining number of the enemy at large and then close with an outline of a campaign plan that he thought would result in final victory?

Carson the Starver of Thousands

Another fault of Trafzer's book is exaggeration. For example, he recognizes that the success of Carson's campaign turned upon destroying Navajo crops and says that this strategy "would result in the starvation of thousands of men, women, and children of the Navajo tribe."[24] Trafzer presents no evidence to support his claim that "thousands" died of starvation, and it appears highly suspect in light of the facts. At the outset of the campaign, Navajo tribal strength was estimated at twelve thousand. By late 1864, 8,354 were living in the Bosque Redondo.[25] This would leave 3,646 unaccounted for. According to Navajo headman Herrera, about 480 Navajo were still at large in their old haunts, including Manuelito's band.[26] That would leave 3,166 unaccounted for. According to the mid-1864 report of Captain P.W.S. Plympton, "some 3,000 Navajos were still living west of the Hopi villages and south of the Little Colorado River in Apache territory."[27] If that report was accurate, it would account for roughly the remainder of the Navajo tribe.

Important too is the charge by Dr. Michael Steck, superintendent of Indian Affairs for New Mexico, "that the Navajo campaign had been a failure because it had not brought in more than half of the Navajos."[28] Even though all of these figures are questionable except for the number actually living in the Bosque, they give us good grounds for being suspicious of Trafzer's assertion that "thousands" died of starvation. A small number of Navajo were killed in the Navajo campaign, and doubtless some did die of exposure and privation during the conflict; that is the extent of the known casualties in the last Navajo war. Because these meager totals make rather unsensational reading, Trafzer seems to have resorted to unsubstantiated exaggeration in his attempt to defame Carson's character.

It is also clear that Trafzer wants the reader to believe that there was something morally wrong with Carson's elimination of the Navajo food supply, when in fact the destruction of an army's supply base is an acceptable tactic in a just war. And because members of the army lived with the civilians, destroying the farmers' food supply was of necessity to destroy the army's food supply. Further, Carson's "scorched earth" policy can be seen as really rather humanitarian — it was better for Carson to destroy the Navajo crops and force them to surrender than for him to have killed them outright.

Carson the Killer of Innocents

Another of Trafzer's charges is that Carson's "campaign failed to distinguish between 'hostiles and friendlies.' "[29] Trafzer accuses Carson of wantonly killing innocent Navajo who were not on the warpath and damns him for failing to distinguish hostile from peaceful Navajo. Such a criticism is easy to make from an armchair, but it ignores the logistical impossibility of making such a distinction, a fact well understood by both Carson and Carleton. Two Navajo peace chiefs, Delgadito and Barboncito, had explicitly asked if they could remain in their old country if they kept the peace. Carleton told them "no" and made clear his reasons why in a dispatch to Lt. Colonel Francisco Chavez: "You remember what I told Barboncito and Delgadito about what would be required of all Navajoes who did not want to engage in the war, or be sufferers from it. That while hostilities were progressing against their tribe no peace party of Navajoes could remain in the country. . . . That we have no desire to make war upon them and other good Navajoes, but the troops cannot tell the good from the bad; and we neither can nor will tolerate their staying as a peace party among those against whom we intend to make war."[30] Hostile Indians did not wear special uniforms. What would Trafzer have had Carson do — ride down a Navajo band, ask them if they were friendly, and if they said "no," commence a firefight? As Carleton said, "the troops cannot tell the good from the bad." Official policy had to insist, therefore, that all who did not want war had to surrender and emigrate so that they would not be caught up in the coming conflict. If they did not emigrate, they were to be considered at war and treated accordingly. Trafzer's criticism ignores the reality of the situation in which Carson was forced to operate.

Trafzer extends this line of criticism in recounting two of Carson's encounters with Navajo farmers. In the first incident, Carson's men discovered and destroyed several acres of grain. They then set an ambush for the growers. When two of these returned, they were shot and wounded but were still able to escape. Carson expressed dismay that they got away, and Trafzer remarks that "Such comments demonstrate how Carson's campaign failed to distinguish between 'hostiles and friendlies.' "[31] On what grounds does Trafzer assume that these farmers were friendlies? Just because they were farmers doesn't mean that they weren't also warriors. Furthermore, those who supply food for troops are legitimate targets in a just war. Trafzer makes it appear that this incident is to Kit's discredit, when in fact it was a perfectly defensible act, given the situation.

Soon after that incident, Kit found and destroyed another large cornfield, but he could locate no Navajo. Of the absent Indians Trafzer says, "They rightfully feared that they would be murdered as the Navajo farmers south of the cañon had been."[32] Soldiers kill other soldiers while murderers kill innocent victims. Trafzer provides no evidence that the farmers in question were innocent. Furthermore, food supplies were shared by warriors and civilians alike. Because the former lived with the latter, to supply food was to be supplying food for the warriors. That they had not surrendered was de facto evidence that they were hostile and subject to being killed if found by Carson's command. To say this would have been murder is linguistic legerdemain. One also wonders how Trafzer knows what the Indians did or did not fear. We have no record of their emotional reaction to the situation.

When Trafzer criticizes Carson for attacking all Navajo "regardless of whether individual Navajos were inclined toward peace or war,"[33] he simply ignores the reality of the situation; it would have been impossible for Carson to determine whether a particular Navajo was for peace or war. To attempt to make such a determination would have unnecessarily exposed his own troops to danger. Trafzer also makes the mistake of assuming that all Navajo who fled were, by definition, not hostile. He says that Carson's troops attacked bands who "were trying to make their escape from the troops, for they had no quarrel with the Bilagaana and did not care to fight."[34] That such bands did not care to fight does not mean that they were peaceful. In all cases where they were confronted with superior force, Navajo policy was to flee. It is an error in logic to assume that because a band fled they were friendly. In fact, *all* bands that Carson encountered fled, proving that flight was no ground for considering a band peaceful.

Near the end of his book, Trafzer remarks that although Carson is a hero to many, "He is remembered as the man who murdered many innocent Navajos, people who had played no role in the hostilities before 1863."[35] Trafzer provides no evidence to back up the assertion that peaceful Navajo were killed, nor does he provide any evidence that those who were killed "had played no role in the hostilities before 1863." And again, given Carleton's ultimatum that all who wanted peace had to surrender and emigrate, Carson had to consider all Navajo remaining in Navajo country hostile. To blame him for acting otherwise is the criticism of an armchair professor, not a person familiar with military reality or the reality of the Navajo War.

Carson the Killer of Women and Children

Trafzer insists that Carson's "war was pursued against all Navajo — men, women, and children — indiscriminately."[36] In considering this charge, it will be helpful to clarify official policy, which was the same in both the Mescalero and Navajo campaigns. Carleton explicitly told Carson that "All Indian men of that tribe are to be killed whenever and wherever you can find them: the women and children will not be harmed, but you will take them prisoners and feed them."[37] Official policy was to kill only the men, taking women and children prisoner. At no time was Carson ordered, and at no time did he make it field policy, to attack men, women, and children "indiscriminately." It is true that a few women and children were killed in the heat of battle, but this was an inevitable consequence of pursing military action against a people whose women and children were mixed in with the warriors. The canons of just warfare preclude *targeting* noncombatants but recognize that some may die as an inevitable consequence of war. The facts are clear that Carson's troops did not target women and children, and Carson's views on those who did are well summed up in his response to the Chivington massacre: "I tell ye what; I don't like a hostile Red Skin any better than you du [sic]. And when they are hostile, I've fit 'em — fout 'em — as hard as any man. But I never yit drew a bead on a squaw or papoose, and I loathe and hate the man who would. 'Taint nateral for brave men to kill women and little children, and no one but a coward or a dog would do it."[38] Official policy was to kill only male warriors, Carson's personal philosophy opposed killing women and children, and no evidence exists to convict Carson of deliberately killing noncombatants. Trafzer's attempts to make this argument run are simply false and unsupported.

Nor should we forget that Carson explicitly disobeyed Carleton's order to kill all Indian men of the tribe "whenever and wherever you can find them." Carson allowed all Navajo — men, women, or children — who wished to surrender to do so. His compassionate nature simply would not allow him to carry out Carleton's ruthless order to kill all the Navajo men whenever and wherever they were found. I think it is fair to say that the Navajo would have fared far worse had an officer who lacked Kit's sensitivity to and sympathy with native culture been in charge. The Navajo were *fortunate* that it was Carson commanding the troops sent against them.

Carson the Brutal Tactician

Another of Trafzer's indictments blames Carson's "ruthless" initial conduct of the war for the Navajos' fear of surrendering. He says, "Carson had initially helped bring on this situation by killing or attempting to kill every warrior he encountered without thought of peace councils. By the winter of 1863, Kit was slowly changing his policy, giving some thought to the possibility of talking with Navajos about their surrender and their removal."[39] The key issue here is Trafzer's assertion, with respect to the conduct of the war, that "Kit was slowly changing his policy." Trafzer insists that Carson initially followed a policy of killing all Navajo on sight, making no attempt to parley, and as the campaign progressed, Carson shifted to a policy of attempting to talk the Navajo into surrendering. According to Trafzer, it was this shift in policy that led to wholesale Navajo capitulation during the Canyon de Chelly expedition. The issue is important because, if Trafzer is right, then Carson bears responsibility for initially pursuing a policy that "caused needless bloodshed, prolonged the war, and convinced the Navajos that Red Clothes' campaign was a war of extermination."[40] The facts do not support Trafzer's assertion.

Two issues here require attention. First, why were the Navajo fearful of surrendering, to what extent did the behavior of Carson's men cause this fear, and must Carson take personal responsibility for Navajo fearfulness? Second, did Carson change his policy toward the Navajo during the conduct of the campaign, a change that made the Navajo more inclined to surrender?

To get at the first issue, we need better to understand why the Navajo feared surrendering. I have already discussed a primary origin of this fear: Blakeney's treachery in killing the emissaries of Herrera Grande who tried to surrender at Fort Canby in August 1863. Convinced by this act that Carson's was a war of extermination, the Navajo were justifiably wary of surrendering — despite Carleton's promise that the consequence of capitulation would simply be removal to the Bosque Redondo.

Carson himself was extremely angry about Blakeney's conduct precisely because Carson understood that it would inhibit Navajo surrender. Kelly aptly says that, "Carson bitterly resented Blakeney's treatment of the prisoners, both because he believed the deaths were unnecessary and because he believed the killings would have a detrimental effect on other Navajos who wished to surrender."[41] For this reason, Carson wrote to Carleton: "I cannot but regret that they were not better received (when received at all) and kept until my arrival."[42]

Other actions of Carson's troops heightened the Navajo's fear of surrendering. A good example is the attempt, apparently by the great chief Manuelito himself, to try to parley with Carson. Kit relates the story to General Carleton:

> The mounted party while out Scouting that day had two horses give out, and when the riders were returning to camp they passed three concealed Indians, one of whom fired off his Rifle in the air, and then rode towards them. On his approach the soldiers were going to shoot him, but owing to his gesticulating they allowed him to draw nigh. He had two Rifles on his saddle, both of which the Soldiers took, after which they allowed him to depart as he came. One of the Rifles was recognized by the Moquis as belonging to Manuelita [sic],a chief of great influence. It is more than

probable that the Indian, whoever he was, desired to have an interview with me but was deterred by the hostile attitude of the Soldiers.[43]

The upshot of Blakeney's killing the prisoners and the soldiers' "hostile attitude" was the Navajo decision to flee from Carson's troops rather than risk surrender. Convinced that surrender would lead to extermination rather than simply relocation, the Navajo whom Carson initially encountered did everything possible to keep from falling into his hands. Carson himself clearly understood why and explained the situation to Carleton: "I cannot blame these people for distrusting the good faith of the Troops at this Post, from the manner in which their Messengers have been received at it on more than one occasion; I deplore it the more as I have only one way of communicating with them — through the barrels of my Rifles."[44] Because the Navajo fled from Carson's troops, verbal exchanges were impossible. Firing on the enemy in flight became the only means of "communication."

Although Carson accepted the responsibility of his command for this situation, we should bear in mind that the fault lies with Blakeney and other subordinates, not with Carson himself. Of course, Carson as field commander had ultimately to take responsibility for the actions of his men, actions that he himself deplored. In Kit's defense, frontier soldiers were not the easiest lot to control. As Utley and Washburn point out, "The regular army contained some able and dedicated soldiers, but in sum they barely achieved a rating of mediocre. The enlisted soldiers were . . . too often criminals, toughs, drunkards, and fugitives swept up from the streets of the big eastern cities by industrious recruiting. . . . And for the officers . . . slow promotion, isolation, boredom, and whiskey dulled ambition."[45] In fact, repeatedly throughout the Navajo campaign, Carson had serious disciplinary problems. Kelly says that although Carson himself had an "essentially compassionate attitude towards the Indians," it was often "negated by the actions of his men, whom he never succeeded fully in controlling."[46] Concerning Carson's men, Kelly continues, "Murder, alcoholism embezzlement, sexual deviation, desertion, and incompetence were all to hamper Carson's conduct of the campaign. Although only one of his officers would be killed by the enemy, almost half of them would be forced to resign in disgrace or face court-martial proceedings before the campaign was over."[47] Thus, although it is true that Carson's troops did take actions that thwarted Navajo surrender, the facts exonerate Carson, at least personally.

The deeper question is the second: Did Carson change his policy toward the Navajo during the campaign, a change that made the Navajo more inclined to surrender? Trafzer asserts that Carson's ruthless initial military policy exacerbated the Navajo fearfulness that had been caused by the misbehavior of his men. Because Carson began his campaign by "initially killing or attempting to kill every warrior he encountered without thought of peace councils," because he refused to give the Navajo a chance to parley, he reinforced their belief that he was waging a war of extermination. According to Trafzer, in the latter stages of the campaign, Carson abandoned this unduly harsh policy in favor of one that depended upon "talking with Navajos about their surrender and their removal."

Did Carson's policy change? Not according to Kelly, who says, "Throughout the campaign Carson's policy was to talk to prisoners about the necessity of emigrating to the Bosque Redondo and then send some of them back to their people."[48] The evidence bears Kelly out. For example, when Carson returned to Fort Canby from his first scout in August 1863, he found at the post an old Indian named Little Foot, whom Blakeney had imprisoned when Little Foot came in to inquire about surrendering his band. Carson personally interrogated Little Foot and learned that his people were prepared to comply with Carleton's wishes. Carson informed the general, "I believe him to have spoken in good faith, and have set him at liberty, giving him twelve days to return with his people, at which time he promises to be here."[49] This incident occurred during the first month of the campaign.

Two months later, Captain Rafael Chacon, post commander at Fort Wingate, followed Carson's lead when Sordo and Pedro Sarracino came in to camp to inquire about terms of surrender. They were neither imprisoned nor killed but rather were allowed to return to their people on the Gallina (a waterhole near Fort Wingate) to await General Carleton's answer to their request to remain in Navajo country "to arrest all delinquents of their tribe, or to fight against them in company with the troops."[50] Although Carleton emphatically said "no," the incident illustrates that the official policy was to send emissaries of peace back to their tribe in an attempt to persuade them to surrender.

In early December, a month before the Canyon de Chelly expedition, Carson informed Carleton that he had released a Navajo boy captured on a scout "that he might communicate to the Navajoes the intentions of the General Commanding in regard to them, of which I took particular pains to inform him."[51] Both early and late in the campaign, Carson's policy remained the same: send captives back to their band to inform the other members of government policy and the consequences of disobeying it. Nor should we forget the emissary work done by peace chief Delgadito. Not long after his surrender and transfer to the Bosque in November 1863, Carleton sent Delgadito back to Navajo country to persuade others to surrender.

That there aren't more examples of captives returned to their bands is due not to a change in Carson's policy but rather to the fact that, initially at least, he rarely encountered any Navajo. When he did, they fled, firing on the troops to cover their escape. The result was that Carson had no opportunity to communicate his intentions directly to the Navajo. Carson's dispatches are filled with reports of the Navajo melting into the fastness of Dinetah (the Navajo's name for their country), giving him no chance to hold "peace councils" with them. Furthermore, the poor condition of his animals as well as the fact that the enlisted men were afoot, often in deep snow, and operating in unfamiliar territory, made overtaking the fleeing Indians difficult, if not impossible. As Kelly says of Carson's November scout west of the Hopi villages, "although he inflicted no great injury, he did encounter more bands of Navajos than he had on previous occasions. Several times he was certain he could have captured or killed the fleeing Indians had his horses been in better shape."[52]

How could Carson have held "peace parleys" with Indians who fired on his troops as he approached and then dispersed and fled? You can't hold peace councils with people who are shooting at or fleeing from you, especially when the poor condition of your horses makes it difficult to pursue them effectively. Carson's only recourse was to destroy their supplies and force them into a situation where they would have to listen. The Canyon de Chelly expedition did just that.

The Scout to Canyon de Chelly

Kelly observes that the Canyon de Chelly expedition was important because it afforded Carson the opportunity "for the first time in the campaign, to confront a sizable number of Navajos face-to-face and to explain to them that emigration to the Bosque Redondo and not extermination was his goal."[53] The key to the Navajo campaign is understanding that prior to the Canyon de Chelly expedition, the Indians themselves were unwilling to parley. This was due in part to their fear that it would do no good, that they faced a campaign of extermination, but also because they saw no need to parley — they felt themselves secure in Canyon de Chelly and saw no need to capitulate to Carson's troops.

The importance of Kit's scorched earth campaign lay in its creation of sufficient duress to force the Navajo to talk and to learn the conditions of surrender. Before the Indians began to feel the effects of Carson's campaign, they were unwilling to parley. By the time Kit entered Canyon de Chelly, the Navajo were desperate and were forced to begin thinking about surrender. Carson's campaign succeeded by drastically altering the mental and physical condition of the Navajo, transforming them from fed, proud, defiant warriors who felt secure in Canyon de Chelly into hungry, humble, harassed, and homeless fugitives. The message of surrender preached by Carson early in the campaign fell on ears unwilling to listen. By mid-winter, however, the specter of death forced the Navajo to begin heeding Carson's message.

Thus the wholesale surrender of the Navajo was caused not by a change in Carson's policy, as Trafzer would have us believe, but rather by a change in the condition of the Navajo. Kit changed neither his policy nor his thinking; he forced the Indians to change theirs. Trafzer says, "The significance of the Cañon campaign came from Carson's success in talking to the Diné and demonstrating that his policy was not to murder them in cold blood."[54] Carson's success in the Cañon campaign came not because he began to talk to the Indians but rather because the Indians were now forced to listen to him. As he wrote to General Carleton after his January foray into Canyon de Chelly,

> It is to the ulterior effects of the "Expedition" that I look for the greatest results. We have shown the Indians that in no place, however formidable or inaccessible, in their opinion, are they safe from the pursuit of the troops of this command; and have convinced a large portion of them that the struggle on their part is a hopeless one. We have also demonstrated that the intentions of the Government toward them are eminently humane; and dictated by an earnest desire to promote their welfare; that the principle is not to destroy but to save them, if they are disposed to be saved.[55]

Carson's personal contact with those who risked surrender convinced the Indians that removal to the Bosque, not extermination, was the goal of the campaign. Kelly explains, "Suffering from exposure and starvation as a result of Carson's earlier forays (which, by the way, were far more effective than Carson ever dreamed), but fearful for their lives because of treatment accorded to captives early in the campaign, the Navajos were already disposed to surrender. What was needed to translate this disposition into action was not an additional show of force but assurance from someone in authority that their trust would not be betrayed."[56]

As Carson encountered the few who risked surrender, he treated them kindly and encouraged them to take advantage of government offers of food, clothes, and protection. Carson's good reputation among the Indians encouraged them to trust his word and to risk surrender. Success in the Navajo campaign depended, then, first upon creating conditions that would dispose the Navajo to listen and second, upon someone of Kit's reputation providing them assurances that the government's intentions were humane. Perhaps Kit Carson alone, of all of the military men in the territory, had both the fighting prowess and the personal reputation to accomplish both of these objectives.

Trafzer, of course, must be critical of Kit Carson, beclouded as he is by Navajo oral history. Harvey Carter and Thelma Guild provide us with an apposite warning concerning that oral history: "Having no written language, the Navajos were inclined to be very creative and dramatic in dealing with their past. Their tribal memory of the events of 1863 and 1864 transformed Carson into a symbol of evil, the cause as well as the agent of the sufferings they endured before, during, and after the Long Walk to the Bosque."[57] What Carter and Guild say of "creative" Navajo oral history applies with equal force to Clifford Trafzer: "It is quite understandable that the Navajos should resent and condemn the destruction of their food supply and their forced removal from their homeland. This does not give them the right, however, to distort history by attributing policies and actions to Carson which were not his at all."[58]

Conclusion

I lament the fact that westward white expansion took the bloody turns that it did. History could have occurred differently had both whites and Indians had different cultural assumptions. It is interesting to imagine what history would have been like if the Europeans who came to the Americas had been religiously tolerant, had taken only land paid for at fair prices, had shared their knowledge with the Indians and borrowed Indian knowledge in return, and had regarded Indian traditions as worthy of respect and understanding. Indian tribes could have been different too. They could have been peaceful groups that did not base their societies on militarism, tribal hatreds, and a strict code of reprisal and retaliation. Had both Indians and whites had different cultural assumptions, the past five hundred years could have been ones of mutual benefit and cultural coexistence. But they weren't, and both sides governed their behavior according to cultural assumptions that virtually guaranteed conflict.

The details of that conflict have now been laid bare and have left deep-seated anger and suspicion. That is not a good formula for future coexistence. To move beyond the present animosity, both sides need to condemn the dehumanization that Indians and whites deteriorated to in the name of their cultural assumptions. We must condemn white culture for perceiving Indians as inferior savages who could be preserved only by confining them and teaching them agriculture and Christianity, for insisting that Indians had to change, and justifying the insistence upon that change by recourse to the concept of a divine Providence that intended the white race to civilize the new world.

We must also condemn Navajo culture for perceiving all those who were not Diné as culturally justified prey for their aggressive and thieving impulses. From 1785 forward, Navajo culture moved more and more toward warfare and raiding — a cultural adaptation that proved highly successful and led to a substantial population increase during the early part of the nineteenth century. Population growth on both sides admixed with diametrically opposed cultural assumptions justifying conflicting behaviors made a bloody showdown almost inevitable.

Instead of nurturing animosities born of that showdown, let us use examples of the unacceptable actions on both sides as guides for how not to behave ever again. And mindful of the faults of our ancestors both red and white, let us try to make the next five hundred years more like the fable of history outlined here.

Finally, I want to conclude with a thought that Marc Simmons will develop more fully in chapter 4. One of the things that I find most admirable in native culture is the willingness to honor and respect individuals of nobility, whether they be friend or foe. In light of that principle, consider these words of Oscar Lipps. Lipps knew personally, for a long time, the elders in the Navajo tribe who actually lived through the last great Navajo war, the Long Walk, the Bosque Redondo, and the return to Dinetah. Writing in 1909, Lipps said, "The name of Kit Carson is to this day held in reverence by all the old members of the Navajo tribe. They say he knew how to be just and considerate as well as how to fight the Indians."[59]

May I suggest that contemporary members of the great Navajo Nation adopt toward Kit Carson the attitude that seems to have been held by their ancestors who actually knew and fought against him — that if they had to be defeated, at least it was by a man of courage and honor, a man who knew their ways and respected them as a people, and whom, in return, they honored with the highly symbolic name Ahdilohee, "The Rope Thrower."

NOTES

1. Clifford E. Trafzer, *The Kit Carson Campaign: The Last Great Navajo War* (Norman: University of Oklahoma Press, 1990), p. xv.
2. Ibid., p. 59.
3. Ibid., p. 6.
4. Ibid., p. 12.
5. Ibid., p. 6.
6. Ibid., p. 118.
7. Lynn R. Bailey, *The Long Walk: A History of the Navajo Wars, 1846–1868* (Los Angeles: Westernlore Press, 1964), p. 145.
8. For Canby's role, see Lawrence C. Kelly, *Navajo Roundup: Selected Correspondence of Kit Carson's Expedition Against the Navajo, 1863–1865* (Boulder, Colo.: The Pruett Publishing Company, 1970), p. 3.
9. Ibid., p. 7.
10. Edwin L. Sabin, *Kit Carson Days 1809–1868: "Adventures in the Path of Empire,"* Volume 2, (New York: The Press of the Pioneers, Inc., 1935), pp. 834–835.
11. Kelly, *Navajo Roundup*, p. 15.
12. Ibid., p. 21.
13. Thelma S. Guild and Harvey L. Carter, *Kit Carson: A Pattern for Heroes* (Lincoln: University of Nebraska Press, 1984), p. 231.
14. Kelly, *Navajo Roundup*, p. 97.
15. Trafzer, *Kit Carson Campaign*, p. 59.
16. Ibid.
17. Kelly, *Navajo Roundup*, pp. 32–33.

18. Ibid., p. 35.
19. Ibid., p. 36.
20. Ibid., p. 69.
21. Ibid., p. 77.
22. Ibid., p. 141.
23. Ibid.
24. Trafzer, *Kit Carson Campaign*, p. 80.
25. Kelly, *Navajo Roundup*, p. 163.
26. Ibid., p. 166.
27. Ibid., p. 161.
28. Ibid., p. 164.
29. Trafzer, *Kit Carson Campaign*, p. 87.
30. Kelly, *Navajo Roundup*, pp. 20–21.
31. Trafzer, *Kit Carson Campaign*, p. 87.
32. Ibid., p. 89.
33. Ibid., p. 97.
34. Ibid., p. 144.
35. Ibid., p. 237.
36. Ibid., p. 87.
37. Kelly, *Navajo Roundup*, p. 11.
38. Sabin, *Kit Carson Days*, Volume 2, p. 765.
39. Trafzer, *Kit Carson Campaign*, p. 131.
40. Ibid., p. 167.
41. Kelly, *Navajo Roundup*, p. 47.
42. Ibid., p. 43.
43. Ibid., p. 76.
44. Ibid., p. 84.
45. Robert M. Utley and Wilcomb E. Washburn, *Indian Wars*, (Boston: Houghton Mifflin Company, 1987), p. 170.
46. Kelly, *Navajo Roundup*, p. 3.
47. Ibid., p. 15.
48. Ibid., p. 47.
49. Ibid., p. 43.
50. Ibid., p. 58.
51. Ibid., p. 77.
52. Ibid., p. 72.
53. Ibid., p. ii.
54. Trafzer, *Kit Carson Campaign*, p. 167.
55. Kelly, *Navajo Roundup*, p. 100.
56. Ibid., p. ii.

57. Guild and Carter, *Pattern for Heroes*, pp. 248–249.
58. Ibid., p. 291.
59. Oscar H. Lipps, *A Little History of the Navajos*, (Cedar Rapids, Iowa: The Torch Press, 1909), p. 59.

CHAPTER 3

The Historiography of the Navajo Roundup

LAWRENCE C. KELLY

This essay reviews the bibliography on Kit Carson and the Navajo Roundup in the belief that it will assist readers to understand how interpretations about the campaign have evolved. Building upon this historiographical essay, I will then offer some remarks on Clifford E. Trafzer's and Lynn Bailey's interpretations of the campaign, indicate how they differ from mine, and speculate on why and how these differences have been occasioned.

My research and writing of *Navajo Roundup: Selected Correspondence of Kit Carson's Expedition Against the Navajo, 1863–1865* took place from 1965 to 1968. At that time there were relatively few reliable scholarly publications on Kit Carson, although, as Darlis Miller points out in chapter 1, there was no dearth of popular, misinformed, and erroneous publications. There were in fact, only six books that I considered potentially valuable:[1] Edwin L. Sabin, *Kit Carson Days, 1809–1868: Adventures in the Path of Empire*; Milo M. Quaife, editor, *Kit Carson's Autobiography*; Bernice Blackwelder, *Great Westerner: The Story of Kit Carson*; M. Morgan Estergreen, *Kit Carson: A Portrait in Courage;* Lynn R. Bailey, *The Long Walk: A History of the Navajo Wars, 1846–1868*; and Harvey L. Carter, *Dear Old Kit: The Historical Christopher Carson.*[2]

The Quaife and Carter books were both annotated versions of Carson's memoirs, dictated in 1856, well before the Navajo campaign began. Although neither of these books was directly helpful in writing my account of the Navajo campaign, there is no doubt that their approving portraits of Carson affected my initial attitude toward him. The memoirs themselves establish Carson's reputation as a modest man, one of few words, a frontiersman whose entire life was spent in the West, where his activities necessarily impinged upon the claims of its native inhabitants. The memoirs also clearly reveal Carson's attitude toward the American Indians, one well formed before he was called upon to lead the Navajo campaign. Quaife quotes Carson as saying: "As long as these mountain Indians are permitted to run at large this country will always remain in its impoverished state, and the only remedy is to compel them to live in settlements, cultivate the soil, and learn to gain their maintenance independent of the general government."[3]

For Carson, as for nearly all members of the dominant white race, Indians would have to make room for the invading whites, eventually abandon hunting, and take up farming. The memoirs also reveal a man who respected Indians in friendly encounters but who would fight to defend what he perceived as his and who was not averse to assisting the army in tracking down any Indian suspected of frontier crimes. At the same time, as both Quaife and Carter note, although Carson twice lived with Indian women in common-law relationships and fathered two children by his first Indian "wife," he was unwilling to acknowledge those relationships in his memoirs.

I found the two Carson biographies by Blackwelder and Estergreen of little use. Neither devotes much space to the Navajo Roundup, and neither contains citations to sources for events described in the text. Estergreen's account of the Navajo campaign appears to rely heavily upon Sabin's study of Carson and the sources he employed. In her notes Blackwelder indicates that she examined original sources in the National Archives and the Library of Congress, but I could not determine that these sources in any way modified previous accounts of the Navajo campaign, nor does she cite these original sources. Both biographies, as their titles indicate, are laudatory of Carson.

Only the Sabin and Bailey books were instructive to my task. Sabin's two-volume biography, a considerable revision of his original 1912 edition, was particularly relevant, for he was the first person to identify printed government documents pertaining to the Navajo campaign, thereby providing important detail derived from official, contemporary records. He even went so far as to reproduce some of those documents in an appendix, an idea that I found attractive. Thus, some selected correspondence from *The Records of the Rebellion* and *The Conditions of the Indian Tribes*[4] had been made available to the reading public several years before I began my research. In *The Long Walk*, Lynn Bailey took the next step by consulting the original records. I have never been able to determine if Bailey actually went to the National

Archives to search for the original documents or whether, as he seems to imply in his introduction, he relied upon copies made by the Navajo Tribal Land Claims Office. In any event, although he apparently missed many of the letters written by Carson and other members of his command and relied mainly upon the two published collections used by Sabin, Bailey's *The Long Walk* presented the most complete account of the Navajo Roundup to the year 1964.

As the full title of his book indicates, Bailey was interested in creating a broad context within which to place his interpretation of the Long Walk. He begins with American occupation of the Southwest in 1846 and only in chapter 8, as he approaches the end of the book, does he commence his account of the Carson campaign. Following this relatively short chapter, the remainder of his book is devoted to the Navajo ordeal in the Bosque Redondo, a topic to which he returned in 1970. Bailey correctly pointed out that the most important result of Carson's seemingly futile campaign during the summer and fall of 1863 was "the destruction of virtually all Navajo fields and planting grounds within a forty mile radius of Cañon Bonito."[5] In *Indian Slave Trade in the Southwest*,[6] he was also the first to demonstrate the significance of Hispanic slave raids against Indian communities in the Southwest and to stress the strength of Navajo raiders against the Hispanic communities along the Rio Grande during the interval between the end of the Canby campaign in the spring of 1861 and the launching of Carson's campaign in the summer of 1863.

Although Bailey's account is more complete than Sabin's — and was the first to express sympathy for the Navajos — I found some aspects of his interpretation difficult to accept. My difficulties began with his frequent claims that the army's strategy, beginning with the Canby campaign in 1860 and continued under Carson's, was to "ruthlessly" burn all Navajo fields in a deliberate "scorched earth" campaign and to slaughter all their domestic animals.[7] He also repeats the legend that Carson's forces destroyed the peach orchards in the Canyon de Chelly during Carson's January 1864 foray. I was also disturbed by his allegations that the troops who escorted the Navajos on the difficult overland journey to the Bosque Redondo shot those who became too weak to continue the journey.[8] All of these statements either bore no citations to documents, or the citations failed to confirm the allegation.[9]

When I began my research in the National Archives and the Library of Congress in the summer of 1965, I was determined to do two things: to scour the archival records from 1862 to 1866 in order to identify all correspondence from Carson and his subordinates to General Carleton and all correspondence from Carleton to his superiors bearing upon the conduct of the Navajo Roundup and, when citing those documents, to supply the complete file number for each so that others would be able to retrace my steps. It was my hope, vain though it has proven to be, to write the definitive account of the Navajo Roundup, thereby correcting the many incomplete or misleading accounts previously published and providing a paper trail to all the pertinent documents so that my account could be easily verified. As I began writing it became increasingly clear that the best way to achieve my goal would be to reproduce many of the documents, so that readers could judge for themselves if the interpretations that I advanced were well grounded. I was fortunate to find a sympathetic editor in Gerald Keenan at Pruett Press.

The interpretations that I offered were relatively few. Carson, I discovered, was a "most reluctant campaigner," who several times attempted to resign his commission in order to return home to his wife and children. He completely misjudged the effects of his early forays during the summer and fall of 1863, and he opposed the winter campaign that broke the Navajo resistance. The penetration of the Canyon de Chelly was not a great "military" victory, as earlier accounts had represented it, nor was Carson knowledgeable about earlier expeditions into the canyon, as Bailey had thought. Despite the orders issued by General Carleton to attack and kill the Navajos "without mercy," Carson on every occasion insisted upon talking to Navajo captives in order to persuade them to emigrate without further bloodshed. On the few occasions that he was successful in talking to captured Navajos, Carson always set them free so that they could spread his word. The great tragedy of the campaign was that Carson's subordinates, whose personalities and actions I attempted to trace in as much detail as I could, thwarted his strategy at almost every opportunity in the early stages of the campaign, thereby prolonging it and compounding the misery of the Navajos who would not surrender until some of them had talked directly to Carson, following the Canyon de Chelly expedition. By that time neither the Navajos nor the army were prepared for the logistical problems that the surrender of thousands of Indians in the dead of winter would present. I found only one instance in which Carson's men ever burned Navajo property and no evidence that Navajos were shot or otherwise mistreated during the Long Walk to the Bosque Redondo, although the accounts of the forced marches indicated clearly the great hardships and the severe loss of life that resulted from moving a people weakened by malnutrition more than four hundred miles in the dead of winter.

Two years after *Navajo Roundup* was published, there appeared the magisterial account of Navajo-white contact from the earliest Spanish contact to 1861 by Frank McNitt, *Navajo Wars: Military Campaigns, Slave Raids, and Reprisals*.[10] Unknown to me, and I presume also to McNitt, was the fact that both of us were working with identical documents on similar topics at approximately the same time. (In his introduction, McNitt states that he spent eight years on his research, from sometime in the early 1960s to 1970–1971.) McNitt's work was, of course, much broader in scope than the relatively modest undertaking I had set for myself. His decision to end his history of the Navajo wars on the eve of the Carson expedition was perhaps occasioned by the publication of my book, which he acknowledged and used. But it is evident that McNitt had examined the correspondence of the Carson campaign, because in 1973, shortly after his death on December 10, 1972, his article entitled "The Long March, 1863–1867" was published in Albert H. Schroeder, editor, *The Changing Ways of Southwestern Indians: A Historic Perspective*.[11] Although there are some small variations in the numbers of Navajos that we identify as having died on the Long Walk, our accounts are strikingly similar, a result that I attribute to the fact that both of us, separately and independently, identified and used the same documents to fashion our narratives. If it is not apparent from what I have already said about McNitt's work, let me state clearly that I have nothing but the highest respect for his account of the Navajo Roundup, and I regard it as independent verification of my own.

The major difference between McNitt's account and mine, one that I regard as most significant, is his painstaking description of the Canby campaign, 1860–1861. Going well beyond earlier accounts, including mine, McNitt established clearly that the Navajo Roundup should not be viewed only in terms of the Carson campaign. Rather, the roundup, especially from the Navajo perspective, should be viewed as having begun with Canby's campaign, when widespread destruction of Navajo crops ushered in what the Navajos call the "Nahondzod — the Fearing Time — an eight year period of death and exile that ended only with their release from captivity at far-off Bosque Redondo."[12] At the end of Canby's campaign, and two years prior to Carson's mission, only wealthy Navajos retained enough livestock to provide minimal food and clothing; "many had died already and many more were near the edges of starvation."[13] Quoting extensively from General Canby's correspondence, McNitt wrote that it was the devastation caused by Canby's campaign, combined with the turmoil in New Mexico occasioned by the outbreak of the Civil War and the fear of a Confederate invasion in the spring of 1861, that opened the door to Hispanic and other Indian raids upon the weakened Navajos. As a result, Canby concluded, there was by 1862 "now no choice between their [the Navajos'] absolute extermination or their removal or colonization at a point so remote . . . as to isolate them entirely from the inhabitants of the Territory."[14] Thus, McNitt reveals that, from the army's perspective, the Navajos' removal was by far the more humane course after 1862. From the time of the Confederate invasion onward, the army was unable to protect the weakened Navajos from their historic foes. However brutal removal may appear to later generations, it was conceived at that time as the better course.

In 1973 the first accounts of the Long Walk to use Navajo oral histories appeared. Crawford R. Buell, a retired Forest Service employee and president of the Santa Fe Historical Society, published "The Navajo 'Long Walk': Recollections by Navajos" in Schroeder's *The Changing Ways of Southwestern Indians: A Historic Perspective.* Although Buell relied only upon published government documents for his narrative and repeated the discredited stories about the burning of Navajo crops and the destruction of their orchards, he revealed one of the sources for the mistaken allegation that Carson's men had destroyed thousands of sheep during their alleged "scorched earth" campaign. That source was John Hanson Beadle's undocumented and hearsay-based account, *The Undeveloped West, or Five Years in the Territories.*[15] Beadle, who had no knowledge of Navajos prior to his travels through the West, which began in 1868, briefly visited Forts Wingate and Defiance between May 31 and June 16, 1871, during which time he learned everything he knew about Navajos from the people he encountered. He does not mention Carson in his one-sentence description of the Navajo Roundup: "In 1863 General W. H. Carleton led an army thither, completely destroyed their means of subsistence, and induced the whole tribe to surrender."[16] On an earlier page he gives a one-paragraph description of Navajo-army relations from 1850 to 1864. In this paragraph he states that there was constant warfare between the Navajos and the army from 1857 to 1864, during which time "The National officers found it impossible to conquer the Navajos except by destroying their stock. It is reported that over fifty thousand sheep were bayoneted. One little valley, a few miles from Defiance, is almost literally paved with the skeletons of sheep destroyed there to prevent the Navajos from using them. The Utes also drove away many thousands, and this tribe was completely beggared. But before they were entirely subjugated, the Texan invasion of 1861–2 took place."[17] Although Beadle's account lacks a sense of precise chronology, I believe it is evident from the passages quoted that if indeed thousands of sheep were killed and left to rot in a valley near Fort Defiance, this slaughter occurred prior to Carson's campaign against the Navajo. Beadle's account was later incorporated into *The Navajo Yearbook, 1951–1961*,[18] a compilation of uneven and uncritical passages pulled together from diverse and often obscure sources as part of the Navajo Tribe's defense of its land claims before the Indian Court of Claims.

Buell also found five Navajo oral histories about the Long Walk, recorded in the 1930s. To my knowledge these were the earliest recorded Navajo oral histories that dealt with the Long Walk. Two of these confirmed that the army provided wagons for the elderly and for children on the Long Walk. Buell also cited accounts by Navajos who testified before the Indian Claims Commission in 1951 that, during the march to the Bosque Redondo, soldiers shot Navajos too weak to walk and forced themselves sexually upon Navajo women. McNitt also cited the testimony of these Navajo witnesses before the Indian Claims Commission in his companion article in Schroeder's collection. Both authors simply reported these accounts without commenting upon their validity.

Also in 1973, Broderick H. Johnson published *Navajo Stories of the Long Walk*,[19] a collection of oral traditions gathered from over forty Navajos in their own language and then transcribed into English. These Navajo recollections, most of them from Navajos aged seventy to ninety, presented a varied and sometimes bewildering account of the Navajo collective memory of the Long Walk. Some of the accounts blamed removal on betrayal by the Enemy Navajos, others upon Navajo brigands, others on the killing of two Mexican boys, several on Navajo slayings of white men bound for California during the 1849 gold rush, and yet others on the government's desire to preserve them from attacks by their Indian neighbors. Some of these accounts say the Navajos were attacked by Carson's men for "no reason at all." Although all accounts of the march substantiate the hardships reported in the dispatches from Carson's men, the details vary widely. Some claim that

Navajos who became too weak to travel, including pregnant women, the old, and the handicapped, were "just shot down" by the troops. Some say that the soldiers provided wagons for the young and the elderly, while others say all were forced to march on foot. Several are accounts by persons whose relatives did not make the march, those whom Carson's troops were unable to capture. Some of these say the Utes were the worst scourge, that they were furnished guns by the army and were promised the Navajos' land as a reward. Many describe the sicknesses experienced by Navajos who were given unfamiliar food on the journey, but the exact cause of illness varies, from bacon to flour to coffee to sugar.

I admit bafflement about the utility or validity of these accounts. Some of these Navajos obviously merged stories from the Spanish and Mexican periods with events that took place after American conquest of the Southwest. One account even merges the alleged destruction of Navajo sheep during the Carson campaign with the sheep reduction program of the 1930s, and many details about Carson's invasion of the Canyon de Chelly are obviously those of the earlier Spanish attacks on Navajos in the Canyon del Muerto. The only conclusion I could draw from these stories is the same one that Ruth Roessel, a Navajo, draws in her preface to the Johnson volume:

> it is obvious . . . that, while the events themselves are vivid and clear in the minds of Navajos even today, time and sequence have become blurred and perhaps confused . . . events that might have been separated by as many as fifty or more years are described as having occurred simultaneously with events that are known to have taken place many years later . . . . these stories reflect an interesting dilemma which in the end goes unresolved. The dilemma concerns who was at fault. Who was basically responsible for the "Long Walk"? These stories, almost without exception, discuss the question, but, if there is any consistency in them, it is the inconsistency regarding places, groups, or people to blame.[20]

I can only conclude that the stories about the killing of captives on the Long Walk, the rape of the women, and the burning of Navajo crops, although possible, are not verifiable. These stories have crept into the literature about the Navajo Roundup simply because they exist and because uncritical authors have failed to identify them as only allegations that cannot be substantiated from any other source.

After the flurry of publications on the Navajo Roundup that appeared between 1970 and 1973, there was a lull until 1976. In that year Gerald

Thompson published *The Army and the Navajos*,[21] which was essentially a history of the Navajo experience in the Bosque Redondo. Skillfully paraphrasing earlier writers and scrupulously citing their works, Thompson's introductory chapter sums up the various army campaigns against the Navajos from 1849 to 1866 before launching into his chosen topic. Carefully reviewing the Canby correspondence that McNitt had emphasized, Thompson likewise concludes that by 1862 the Navajo faced only two choices: extermination or removal. The only places that Thompson's account differs from mine are in his repetition of the charge that Navajo fields had been burned and that the Canyon de Chelly invasion had been a great military victory. In both these cases, he chose to follow Bailey's account.

Three years after Thompson's book, there appeared what I thought would be the final word on the topic: J. Lee Correll's, *Through White Men's Eyes: A Contribution to Navajo History, The Navajo People From Earliest Times to the Treaty of June 1, 1868.*[22] This major undertaking, the publication of all the archival documents collected by the Navajo Tribe for use in its claim before the Indian Claims Commission, made available in published form all the major documents upon which to base a history of the Navajo people through 1868. The editors were exacting in their efforts to identify the archival location of each document they printed, and they were also careful to note their indebtedness to others for those documents that had somehow escaped their researchers and were not part of the tribal archive. These volumes were published without editorial narrative or interpretation. The only caveat presented was the comment that the documents represented "only one side of a situation, and that from the White man's viewpoint." The Navajo side could never be presented except "through oral tradition." For reasons that were not expressed, those oral traditions, as represented in the Johnson collection, were not included in the volumes.

That brings us to 1983 and the publication of Clifford Trafzer's *The Kit Carson Campaign: The Last Great War Navajo War.*[23] Because R. C. Gordon-McCutchan has already provided a critique of the major flaws in Trafzer's book, I will refrain from commenting further on that topic and will instead concentrate on Trafzer's distortions of the historian's craft.

At the time that Trafzer's book first appeared, I questioned whether he had actually consulted the many documents that he cites in his footnotes.[24] For this essay, I re-checked all his footnote citations, beginning with chapter 2, and concluded more emphatically than before that he did not perform the research in the original documents that he claimed to have done. The appropriation of someone else's research without attribution and the attempt to pass it off as one's own was, at least at the beginning of my career as a historian, considered an unprofessional act that called for challenge and exposure. I hasten to add that the misappropriation of someone else's research does not of itself necessarily result in bad history. But when the misappropriation is also coupled with distortion and misrepresentation of the original sources, it does. In my judgment Clifford Trafzer not only appropriated material from Frank McNitt, Lynn Bailey, and myself without attribution, but he also misrepresented the material he appropriated in order to fashion a revisionist interpretation that he had adopted even before he consulted our works. In his cavalier distortion of sources, he has unfairly damned Kit Carson, ill-served the Navajo people, who deserve better than the fictional and stereotypical Indians he has created, and misled the general public. The evidence for this harsh judgment follows.[25]

Allegations Not Substantiated by the Citations

p. 36: "thousands of Indian slaves were taken by New Mexicans and sold into servitude for great profits. . . . Children between five and fifteen years of age brought as much as two hundred dollars on the auction block in Santa Fe." Trafzer's source for this information is given in chapter 1, footnote 31. The three documents cited there say nothing about "thousands of Indians" being enslaved and nothing about an "auction block" in Santa Fe where Indian captives were sold. Instead, the documents substantiate only that an Indian slave trade still existed in the 1850s and that Sandoval, the leader of the Enemy Navajo band, was a major figure in that trade. Trafzer appears oblivious to the irony involved in citing sources that implicate a Navajo in the slave trade. In truth, all parties to Indian-white conflict in New Mexico in the 1850s were involved in slavery, as Bailey and McNitt made clear years ago.

pp. 48, 78, 88, 102: On these pages Trafzer repeats the Bailey version of Carson's burning of Navajo crops during the summer and fall of 1863. All of the letters to which he refers in his footnote were published in their entirety in *Navajo Roundup,* and none of them contain any reference to destruction by burning. Indeed, they state that Carson salvaged much of the grain as feed for his horses later in the year; the remainder was fed to his horses immediately or "destroyed" in an unspecified manner. In all the correspondence describing the Navajo Roundup, there is only one letter that refers to the burning of Navajo property, that of lst Lieutenant Donacio Montoya, December 20, 1863, published in *Navajo Roundup,* pp. 85–87. With regard to that incident, Trafzer claims that Montoya's troops took "trophies" (p. 134), when the document plainly states that all captured articles were burned.

p. 49: Trafzer's account of General Canby's activities in the spring of 1862. The source Trafzer gives for this information (chapter 1, footnote 49), cites Canby's correspondence of January 14; February 6, 27; and March 11, 18, 1861. Trafzer says that these documents are located in the New Mexico Indian Superintendency Records. The correct source for this correspondence, as reported in McNitt's *Navajo Wars,* pp. 412–413, is the National Archives, Record Group 393, Records of the U.S. Army Continental Commands, 1821–1920, Department of New Mexico. Thus, although the information in the text is correct, Trafzer's citation is incorrect, betraying his unfamiliarity with these primary sources.

p. 63: Trafzer describes the killing of two Mescalero Apache leaders, Manuelito and José Largo, by Captain James "Paddy" Graydon. As he does in all his accounts of contact between Indians and the units under Carson's command, Trafzer depicts these Indians as peaceful and honorable victims of army treachery. The available evidence, however, indicates that their motives were at best ambiguous. As a result of his unwarranted assumptions, Trafzer is able to characterize the killing of these two headmen as "murder" committed while the Mescaleros "were seeking peace with the whites." In his footnote to this incident (chapter 2, footnote 12), Trafzer cites only "RG 393, Letters Received" for October 23 and 24, 1862, with no apparent understanding that this incomplete citation (neither the authors of the letters, nor the persons addressed, nor the file number are given) would not enable a reader to check his sources. For a description of the complexity of this encounter and exact citations to all of the sources from which it has been reconstructed, see *Navajo Roundup,* pp. 13–14.

pp. 65–66: Here Trafzer twice quotes General Canby on the condition of the Navajo following his 1860–1861 campaign. His citation (chapter 2, footnote 15), however, is not to Canby's correspondence but to a letter from the New Mexico superintendent for Indian Affairs. His next footnote, number 16, is to a Canby letter in the proper source, RG 393, but it bears no date or file number, again making it impossible to check the accuracy of his quotation.

p. 73: Carson's first attempted resignation from the Navajo campaign, February 3, 1863. Trafzer's citation to this letter (chapter 3, footnote 3) is to RG 94, Records of the Adjutant General's Office. The entire letter is published in *Navajo Roundup,* pp. 15–16, where the correct citation, National Archives, Microcopy M–427, Records of Volunteer Soldiers Who Served in Organizations from the Territory of New Mexico, is given. In this and in later incomplete citations to M–427, it is clear that Trafzer is unfamiliar with this source, although he quotes freely from its documents. To my knowledge, *Navajo Roundup* is the only publication on the Navajo Roundup to use M–427. Given that Trafzer frequently quotes from M–427 documents, yet always cites them incompletely or incorrectly, I question that he has consulted the original documents. The contradiction between his characterization of Carson as a "reluctant campaigner" on this page and his opposite characterizations of Carson (pp. 53, 73) as a man who volunteered for the campaign because he loved excitement, adventure, and the thrills that he derived from "the hardship, danger, and challenge of the big-sky country," should also be noted.

p. 85: Trafzer's account of the death of Major Joseph Cummings. As the source for this passage, Trafzer cites a letter from Carson to Carleton dated April 19, 1863 (chapter 3, footnote 15). There is no such letter. The correct source for part of this passage is a letter from Carson to Carleton, *August 19,* 1863, published in its entirety in *Navajo Roundup,* pp. 36–37. The correct source for the manner of Cummings's death is Cummings's service record in M–427, roll 5; see *Navajo Roundup,* p. 35, text and footnote 19.

pp. 87–89: Trafzer reports that Carson turned over six Navajo women and children, captured during a "scout" in early August 1863, to his Ute spies "as slaves for their 'services.' " Scrutiny of the document he cites as his source (chapter 3, footnote 16) reveals no such information. In *Navajo Roundup* (where the document is printed in its entirety, pp. 38–41), I speculated in footnote 32 (p. 39) that these prisoners had been given to the Utes. It appears that Trafzer simply turned my footnote speculation into a textual fact.

There are additional speculations in this section that have no factual basis. For instance, Trafzer says that Carson did not encounter many Navajos on this scout because they "knew of Carson's presence and chose not to reveal themselves" (p. 89). There is no evidence to indicate why Carson encountered so few Navajos. Trafzer also says that had Carson attempted to dam the streams that flowed into the Canyon de Chelly, "the Navajos would have fought tenaciously to destroy" the dams. These comments are little more than bravado and have no basis in any source.

pp. 98–105: Trafzer describes Carson's second major scout of the campaign. The only source that he cites (chapter 4, footnotes 3–6) is a letter from Carson to General Carleton, October 5, 1863. There is no such letter, but there is a letter from Carson to Carleton's adjutant general, Benjamin C. Cutler, of the same date. It is reproduced in its entirety in *Navajo Roundup,* pp. 53–56. Inserted into Trafzer's text are also several quotations taken from a parallel account of this scout written by Sergeant George W. Campbell. Campbell's report is not cited, but those portions of his correspondence that are quoted have appeared in print only in *Navajo Roundup* (p. 53, text and p. 54, footnote 59).

Trafzer has also misread Carson's report. On p. 102 he says that a party of Navajos attacked Carson's men near Fort Canby, "letting fly their deadly arrows, killing one of the bluecoats and wounding another." What Carson actually wrote was, "They [three men] were attacked by a party of Indians when within five miles of this Post, one of whom they killed. One of the men named Artin, a Private of CO. 'G,' being a little in advance was very severely wounded, though it is expected he will recover." None of Carson's men was killed in this encounter. Nor are the weapons used by the Navajos identified. See *Navajo Roundup,* p. 55.

Trafzer's account, pp. 102–103, of a subsequent encounter between Carson's men and a lone Navajo, is typically romanticized. Carson's description of this event states only that, "On the 3d of October I arrived at the Jarra about 8 miles South of Puebla Colorado. Lieut. Postle here discovered an Indian whom he pursued with six men. Being in advance of his party he overtook the Indian whom he wounded in three places, when he was himself slightly wounded by the Indian." In Trafzer's account, these two sentences are rendered as, "Eight miles south of Pueblo Colorado, at a place called Jarra, six soldiers encountered a lone warrior. As soon as they sighted the Navajo the chase was on, and the soldiers were soon able to overtake the Indian. The blood of many warriors flowed through that Navajo's veins, and he fought fiercely for his life against bad odds. He was wounded three times, but managed to escape nonetheless. Only one soldier was wounded, but all six suffered from embarrassment." See *Navajo Roundup,* p. 55.

pp. 106–108: Footnote 8 cites a letter from McCabe to Murphy, October 12, 1863. This source is correctly identified, but Trafzer omits the necessary additional information that McCabe's letter was an enclosure to Carson's letter of October 20, 1863, and can only be located by a reference to the Carson letter. His citation in footnote 9 is similarly flawed. Here he cites an unsigned letter of October 29, 1863, as "Major Sena to Murphy." In *Navajo Roundup,* p. 68, footnote 86, I argue from internal evidence that the author had to be Sena.

p. 111: In footnote 13, Trafzer identifies the source of Carleton's statement to General Thomas as Carleton to Thomas, December 5, 1863. In fact, the quotation is from Carleton to Thomas, November 22, 1863; see *Navajo Roundup,* p. 71, footnote 92. The only portion of this letter that Trafzer chooses to quote is exactly that portion excerpted in *Navajo Roundup,* except that he has added the word "can," which does not exist in the original.

pp. 112–125: In his description of Carson's scout that began on November 15, 1863, Trafzer becomes particularly inventive. According to him, there was "A cold breeze . . . sweeping the parade ground" as Carson set out (p. 117); Carson "probably destroyed" a group of Navajo "hogans and took any food he found" (p. 117); an encounter between sixty Navajos and the guard at Fort Canby is enlivened by "whizzing arrows" and "the crack of rifles and handguns [that] could be heard for miles, echoing through the rocks and crevices of Cañon Bonito" (p. 118); and Carson becomes "enraged" and "irate" at the incompetence of Major Sena (p. 120). There is no factual basis for any of these statements. For the documents upon which his narrative is based, see *Navajo Roundup,* pp. 70–79 and 84–85, where they are printed in their entirety. The letters from Sena and the AAA General, which he cites incompletely in chapter 4, footnote 18, can only be found as enclosures to other letters, which he does not cite, again giving rise to a suspicion that Trafzer is unfamiliar with the original sources.

p. 160: Trafzer's account of Carson's first contact with a delegation of Navajos following the successful passage through the Canyon de Chelly by Captain Pfeiffer. The citations for this account (chapter 5, footnotes 33–36) are all from Navajo oral histories. Yet, in Carson's report to Carleton, January 24, 1864, which is not cited, Carson wrote that he told the Navajo delegation that they could surrender at any time until the following mid-morning without fear of molestation. However, if they did not present themselves by that time, Carson said, "my soldiers would hunt them up and the work of destruction recommence." Trafzer renders these words as follows: "If they failed to comply with his command, he threatened, he would hunt them down like animals and destroy them unmercifully." Compounding this prejudicial paraphrase, Trafzer also fails to mention that Carson stated that these Navajos told him that they had earlier been informed by "an old captive whom I had sent back to them" that he was only intent upon their immigration to the Bosque Redondo, not on killing them, but they were afraid to believe the message prior to meeting with Carson himself. For the entire letter see *Navajo Roundup,* pp. 98–101.

FABRICATIONS AND DISTORTIONS

p. 50: Referring to the period after Canby's campaign in 1860–1861, Trafzer writes: "The world seemed to be closing in on them, as the food, clothing, and protection promised by the American government were not forthcoming. It seemed to the Navajos that the Bilagaana had lied once again and that their words, as thick as smoke when spoken, had vanished into the air." Aside from the fact that there is no record of what "seemed" to the Navajos to be the meaning of the treaty imposed by Canby, Trafzer's characterization of its terms is totally incorrect. The treaty said nothing about food and clothing but instead stated flatly that Navajos were forbidden to live or graze east of Fort Fauntleroy (the area in which Carson concentrated his initial scouts and in which, Trafzer steadfastly maintains, against the evidence, that all Navajos were peaceful farmers), and it specifically stated in section six that only "Whenever the government of the United States is satisfied that the Navajo people will conform in good faith to the conditions and stipulations of this treaty, put an end to their depredations and live in peace with all their neighbors, measures [will] be taken to render them any assistance that may be necessary to place them in the same condition with other nations." McNitt gives the terms of the treaty on p. 415 of *Navajo Wars;* it is also published in Correll, *Through White Men's Eyes,* vol. 6, pp. 85–90.

pp. 73–75: Trafzer's account of the Navajo delegation that met with General Carleton in December 1862. Trafzer's citation for this encounter is

Carleton's letter to Lorenzo Thomas, March 19, 1863. This letter contains nothing about a meeting with the Navajo headmen (see *Navajo Roundup,* pp. 16–17). Instead, Carleton's description of this meeting (published in *Navajo Roundup,* p. 18), is contained in his report to Thomas of December 20, 1862. More significant is the fact that Trafzer has fabricated his account of the Navajos' representations at this meeting. According to him, the Navajos told Carleton that they could not accept his order to remove to the Bosque Redondo and that they would fight to preserve their "traditional lands," which they held as "sacred. Since the creation of the world, the Navajos said, Dinetah had been theirs and was given to them by the Holy People of the First World. They could not surrender their land and move from it, for to do so would be a violation of their deepest religious beliefs. They chose to fight for what they knew to be theirs." None of this is in the document.

In addition to incorrectly citing the source for this meeting and fabricating a conversation that is not verified in any source, Trafzer also fails to inform his readers that at the meeting, Carleton told the Navajo delegation that "they could have no peace until they would give other guarantees than their word, that the peace should be kept. — To go home and tell their people so. — That we had no faith in their promises. — That if they did not return, we should know they had chosen the alternative of war. That in this event, the consequences rested with them." See *Navajo Roundup,* p. 18. It was, of course, not until after these Navajos failed to return that Carleton instructed Carson to begin the Navajo campaign in the spring of 1863.

p. 80: Trafzer states, without any citation, that Carson's destruction of Navajo crops resulted "in the starvation of thousands of men, women, and children of the Navajo tribe." Surely, the death of so many Navajos (an estimated fifteen percent of the tribe) would have been noted or alleged in some account of the Navajo Roundup, but no one, except Trafzer, has ever before placed the Navajo losses in the "thousands."

pp. 80–81: Here Trafzer states that Carson's Ute allies attacked "without provocation" a small band of "Navajo farmers and their families" who were "peacefully farming" near Fort Defiance. The one source he cites for this incident (chapter 3, footnote 9) contains no phrasing that could lead to these descriptions. It merely reports that "the Utah Indians had preceeded us on this day's march, killed one man (Navajoe) and captured twenty sheep." The full report is in *Navajo Roundup,* pp. 27–28. In this same passage Trafzer remonstrates against Carson's appeal to Carleton to permit the Utes to keep

The Historiography of the Navajo Roundup

their Navajo prisoners, but he makes no mention of the fact that the Navajos had in their possession a Paiute woman.

pp. 137–138: Trafzer's account of the first Navajo prisoners to exhibit deprivation as the result of Carson's earlier campaigns. Here Trafzer quotes Carson as saying that the women and children "must have been without any description of food" for some time. Although the Navajos described by Carson were indeed, in his words, "destitute" and "almost entirely naked," Carson actually wrote that, "had it not been for the unusual growth of the Pinon-berry this year, they must have been without any description of food." See *Navajo Roundup*, pp. 92–94 for Carson's entire letter. Not satisfied with distorting the condition of the captured Navajos, Trafzer then inserts the following imaginary description, which has no basis in any documentary source: "Their bodies were thin, except for their bellies, which were pitifully swollen from malnutrition Their eyes were far back in their heads and were as dark and empty as those of the dead."

Egregious Errors

pp. 67–70: As he concludes his introduction to Carson's Navajo campaign, Trafzer introduces one of the best-known and most reprehensible events in Navajo–U.S. relations, the "massacre" at Fort Fauntleroy in September 1861. This incident, which was first described in *Conditions of the Indian Tribes,* implicated the post commander, Manuel Chavez, who had led numerous volunteer raids against the Navajos in earlier years. It has been analyzed in several publications, most notably in Marc Simmons, "Horse Race at Fort Fauntleroy: An Incident of the Navajo Wars," *La Gaceta* 5 (1970), pp. 3–13, and McNitt, *Navajo Wars,* pp. 421–429, both of which are cited in Trafzer's bibliography. In all of these accounts the 1861 massacre has been interpreted as a major factor in General Canby's decision to remove the Navajo to a distant reservation. Weakened first by Canby's winter campaign in 1860–1861 and then scattered by the Fort Fauntleroy incident, the Navajo had became easy prey for their traditional foes. Facing the threat of a Confederate invasion that necessitated the withdrawal of his troops from the Navajo country, Canby drafted a plan in November 1861 for Navajo removal in order to protect them from raids by Utes and New Mexicans. By changing the date of the Fort Fauntleroy massacre to September 1862, a year later than its actual occurrence, Trafzer arrived at an entirely new, and entirely unfounded, interpretation. According to his account (p. 70), a year of generally peaceful relations between the Navajo and the citizens of New Mexico followed the Canby campaign, from the spring of 1861 until September 1862, when the massacre "ended all chance of a peaceful settlement with the Navajos." Chavez's action, he states, "contributed significantly to starting a new Navajo war that would bring Kit Carson to Dinetah to begin his campaign in the summer of 1863." How someone supposedly familiar with the archival records and the earlier literature about such a well-known event could have so confused its role in Navajo-army relations is difficult to fathom.

p. 83: In discussing Carson's request to permit his Ute allies to keep captured Navajo women and children, a request that Carleton denied, Trafzer writes that Carleton denied the request "not because it was 'most humane and proper,' as he put it, but because it would interfere with his plan to Christianize and 'civilize' his ignorant, 'savage' charges." There are three problems with this rendition of Carleton's words. One is the citation (chapter 3, footnote 10) to Carleton's letter of July 24, 1863, when it should be Carleton to Carson, August 18, 1863, RG 393, Letters Sent, vol. 14, p. 20. Both of these letters were printed in their entirety in *Navajo Roundup,* pp. 30–31. If Trafzer had been working from the original documents, it is most unlikely that he would have confused the two.

The second problem is that there is no mention of "ignorant, 'savage,' charges" in either the letter Trafzer cites or the correct citation. The third, and most flagrant error, is Trafzer's statement that Carleton believed that enslavement was "humane and proper" treatment for Navajos. What Carleton actually said in the letter of August 18, 1863, was: "in relation to the disposition to be made of captured Navajoe women and children [I] say in reply, that *all* prisoners which are captured by the troops or employés of your command will be sent to Santa Fé. . . . Here the Superintendent of Indian Affairs and myself will make such dispositions as to their future care and destination, as may seem most humane and proper." (See *Navajo Roundup,* p. 31.)

p. 199: Lt. George Campbell's account of his expedition to Cubero and Cebolleta to free Navajos held as slaves by New Mexicans. According to Trafzer, Campbell reported that he was able to persuade only "a few of the inhabitants to give up their slaves" and that he was "convinced that he had only secured about half of the number of Navajos held by Hispanos." Campbell's letter is published in its entirety in *Navajo Roundup*, pp. 148–149. In it Campbell states clearly, if illiterately, that he had collected ninety-five Navajos, a number that was more than *twice* as many as he anticipated. Other letters published in *Navajo Roundup*, but ignored by Trafzer, indicate that the army made a concerted effort in 1864 to free Navajos enslaved by New Mexicans.

p. 211: Trafzer's account of a party of Colorado volunteers who were engaged in a raid against the Navajos in the spring of 1864. According to Trafzer, Captain Asa Carey "condoned the actions of this force and even supplied them with government rations." This passage contains several quotations that do not exist in the document Trafzer cites (chapter 7, footnote 16), speculations that have no basis in the document, and the insinuation that women and children were among the Navajos killed by this party. Carey's letter (see *Navajo Roundup*, pp. 130–131) states that the Colorado volunteers, who were "entirely destitute," were issued only enough food to return to Colorado and that all their Navajo prisoners were taken from them. There is no mention of the sex or ages of the Navajos killed. Trafzer also omits earlier correspondence by Carey published in *Navajo Roundup*, pp. 120–125, that demonstrates the captain's efforts to halt volunteer raids while the Navajos were in the process of surrendering.

CONTRADICTIONS AND GRATUITOUS INTERPRETATIONS

p. 75: Trafzer states that Carleton "tried to ensure the success of the expedition by sending Carson out with . . . a competent military staff." He then contradicts himself by proceeding to demonstrate the point I made explicitly in *Navajo Roundup*, namely, that many of Carson's subordinates were incompetent and that it was their incompetence that resulted in the failure of many of Carson's early overtures to the Navajo. The examples that Trafzer gives of Carson's personnel problems (pp. 92–95) are remarkably similar to those recited in *Navajo Roundup*, pp. 44–52.

p. 83: At several places in his account, Trafzer castigates the army for supplying Navajos with flour, with which they were unfamiliar and which made them ill. In this passage, however, he maintains that the Navajos were deprived, as the result of Carson's destruction of their wheat fields, of the necessary "flour for fry bread [which was] an important part of their daily diet." He cannot have it both ways. The documents do indicate that some Navajos became ill during the Long Walk as a result of being supplied with flour, with which they were unfamiliar.

p. 151: Although he uncritically accepted Navajo oral traditions earlier, Trafzer is forced to admit here that those recollections are incorrect about the destruction of the Navajo peach orchards in the Canyon de Chelly during Carson's command. Captain John Thompson destroyed the orchards later, in August 1864. See *Navajo Roundup,* p. 99, footnote 30.

p. 152: Trafzer argues here that, "had the Navajos not been suffering from hunger and cold, they could have prevented Pfeiffer's passage through their stronghold without great difficulty" and that there were "several sites where they could have surprised the invaders and cut them to pieces." These observations are wholly gratuitous and totally at variance with the known facts about the condition of the Navajos at the time Pfeiffer entered the Canyon de Chelly.

The most recent book published on Carson's campaign against the Navajo is Harvey L. Carter and Thelma S. Guild, *Kit Carson: A Pattern for Heroes.*[26] The authors devote one chapter to the Navajo campaign, chapter 18. Most of their citations in this chapter are to *Navajo Roundup;* there is no reference to Trafzer's book. While on his deathbed, Carter wrote to me about the Navajo Roundup debate and said that he and Thelma Guild had been under great pressure from the University of Nebraska Press in 1983 to cut "about sixty pages" from their manuscript, which had been accepted for publication shortly before Trafzer's book appeared. "We were so involved with the cutting," he wrote, that we failed to read Trafzer, or deal with it, or list it." He added that they cited *Navajo Roundup* for the Carson campaign more often than any other source because, having compared the originals to their printed versions in *Navajo Roundup,* "I knew that your study was representative of the only possible conclusion and interpretation. And I believe a secondary author who does that kind of work ought to receive all the credit for it that can be given to him by others when they discover it."

Conclusion

What are we to conclude from this review of the historiography of the Navajo Roundup? It is obvious, I hope, that there are serious differences between Clifford Trafzer's account and my own and less serious differences between Bailey's book and mine. Bailey's book, which has gone though three printings (1964, 1970, and 1978) without any revisions, contains a few errors that have been adversely influential in tarnishing Carson's reputation, but its most serious limitation today is that its early chapters have been supplanted by McNitt's *Navajo Wars,* and its brief account of the Navajo campaign has been supplanted by *Navajo Roundup* and Thompson's *The Army and the Navajos.*

Trafzer's book and mine rely on virtually identical sources; only the interpretations are different. I hope I have made clear how Trafzer, using the same sources I did, was able to arrive at an interpretation so divergent from mine, but if I have not, I invite readers to decide for themselves. Of one thing they can be certain. In *Navajo Roundup* they will find not only my interpretation of the original documents but also the documents themselves — in most cases the entire document — together with full citations to the original's location. It should be relatively easy for any serious reader to determine for him or herself what kind of man Carson was.[27]

Notes

1. In addition to these books, there were several articles, published in *The New Mexico Historical Review* between 1937 and 1953, that I acknowledged in *Navajo Roundup,* p. 174.

2. Edwin L. Sabin, *Kit Carson Days, 1809–1868: Adventures in the Path of Empire,* 2 vols. (New York: The Press of the Pioneers, 1935); Milo M. Quaife, ed., *Kit Carson's Autobiography* (Chicago: The Lakeside Press, 1935); Bernice Blackwelder, *Great Westerner: The Story of Kit Carson* (Caldwell, Idaho: Caxton Press, 1962); M. Morgan Estergreen, *Kit Carson: A Portrait in Courage* (Norman: The University of Oklahoma Press, 1962); Lynn R. Bailey, *The Long Walk: A History of the Navajo Wars, 1846–1868* (Los Angeles: Westernlore Press, 1964); and Harvey L. Carter, *Dear Old Kit: The Historical Christopher Carson* (Norman: University of Oklahoma Press, 1968).

3. Milo Quaife, ed., *Kit Carson's Autobiography,* p. 168. See also Harvey Carter, *Dear Old Kit: the Historical Christopher Carson,* p. 144 for a slightly different version of Carson's statement.

4. U.S. War Department, *The War of the Rebellion: A Compilation of the Official Records of the Union and Confederate Armies,* Series 1, 53 vols. (Washington, D.C.: GPO, 1880–

1901); U.S. Senate, *Condition of the Indians Tribes,* Report of the Joint Special Committee, Senate Executive Document 156, 39 Cong., 2 sess., (Washington, D.C.: GPO, 1867).

5. Bailey, *The Long Walk,* p. 160.
6. Lynn R. Bailey, *Indian Slave Trade in the Southwest: A Study of Slave-Taking and the Traffic in Indian Captives* (Los Angeles: Westernlore Press, 1966).
7. Bailey, *The Long Walk,* pp. 139, 161, 166.
8. Bailey, *The Long Walk,* p. 168.
9. All of these allegations were repeated in Bailey's *Bosque Redondo: An American Concentration Camp,* published in the same year as my *Navajo Roundup,* 1970. See Lynn R. Bailey, *Bosque Redondo* (Pasadena, Calif.: Socio-Technical Books, 1970), pp. 2, 42–43, 54, 56, 149. In *Bosque Redondo,* Bailey also added new charges against the army: flour furnished to the Navajos was "contaminated with rat droppings," p. 55; the army or its auxiliaries were stationed at "all springs and water holes," p. 42; Carson was responsible for unleash[ing] every enemy known to the Dine," p. 2. Unlike *The Long Walk,* Bailey's book on the Bosque Redondo contains no footnote citations to support his statements, and on several occasions it fabricates conversations between the Americans and the Navajos; see especially pp. 35–36.
10. Frank McNitt, *Navajo Wars: Military Campaigns, Slave Raids, and Reprisals* (Albuquerque: University of New Mexico Press, 1972).
11. Albert H. Schroeder, ed , *The Changing Ways of Southwestern Indians: A Historic Perspective* (Glorieta, N.M.: Rio Grande Press, 1973).
12. McNitt, *Navajo Wars,* p. 403.
13. McNitt, *Navajo Wars,* pp. 403, 416.
14. McNitt, *Navajo Wars,* p. 429.
15. John Hanson Beadle, *The Undeveloped West, or Five Years in the Territories* (Philadelphia: National Publishing Co., 1873).
16. Beadle, *Undeveloped West,* p. 530.
17. Beadle, *Undeveloped West,* p. 529.
18. *The Navajo Yearbook, 1951–1961* (Window Rock, Ariz.: Navajo Agency, 1961).
19. Broderick H. Johnson, *Navajo Stories of the Long Walk* (Tsaile, Ariz.: Navajo Community College, 1973).
20. Johnson, *Navajo Stories of the Long Walk,* pp. ix, x.
21. Gerald Thompson, *The Army and the Navajos* (Tucson: University of Arizona Press, 1976).
22. J. Lee Correll, *Through White Men's Eyes: A Contribution to Navajo History, The Navajo People From Earliest Times to the Treaty of June 1, 1868,* 6 vols. (Window Rock, Ariz.: Navajo Heritage Center, 1979).
23. Clifford Trafzer, *The Kit Carson Campaign: The Last Great War Navajo War* (Norman: University of Oklahoma Press, 1982).
24. Lawrence C. Kelly, *Arizona and the West* 25 (1983), pp. 179–180. I was not alone in this position; see Peter Iverson's review in *The American Historical Review* 88 (1983), p. 479. For an example of a reviewer who was taken in by Trafzer's apparent "exhaustive research in original sources," see Robert M. Utley, *The Journal of American History,* 69 (1983), pp. 980–981.

25. In 1993 the *Santa Fe Reporter* published a feature story entitled "The Second Battle for the West," 19 (June 30–July 6, 1993) in which Patricia Limerick was quoted as saying, with reference to the symposium that occasioned this essay: "I don't know why these aging historical figures have to be gussied up. I think Kit Carson would be very angry that these wimpy intellectuals feel it necessary to be defending him." Because I do not know the complete context of her comments to the *Santa Fe Reporter*, I can only hope that she did not mean that incidents of plagiarism and faulty interpretation in revisionist accounts of western history should be ignored or that addressing such topics is not a fit subject for "wimpy intellectuals."
26. Thelma S. Guild and Harvey L. Carter, *Kit Carson: A Pattern for Heroes* (Lincoln: The University of Nebraska Press, 1984).
27. Another alternative would be to consult the Navajo version of the original documents in J. Lee Correll, *Through White Men's Eyes*. Although this version of the original documents was available to Trafzer when he wrote his book, there is no citation to it in his book, although he lists it in his bibliography, where he gives an incorrect date for its publication.

CHAPTER 4

Kit and the Indians

Marc S. Simmons

Kit Carson was a hero and a legend in his own time. That is a fact verifiable by the historical record. Today, on the other hand, he is regarded in many quarters as an archvillain of the American frontier, as an unprincipled exploiter and murderer of Indians. None of the sources that historians rely upon to describe and explain past events sustains that negative view of the man. Nevertheless, the public, having been subjected for twenty years to serious accusations and a barrage of slurs upon his reputation, now firmly believes that Carson was some sort of inhuman monster.

The monster image, growing out of Kit's supposed hatred for Indians and his alleged slaying of masses of them, has not yet been studied in a systematic way. Therefore, in describing its development, one has to pull together an assortment of scattered references in an effort to paint a true picture of what is currently going on. From this exercise, some astonishing things emerge, about our history and about ourselves.

The modern discrediting of Kit seems to have begun in a serious way in the late 1960s and early 1970s, among both Indians and whites. It coincided with the Civil Rights Movement and with the growing disenchantment over the war in Vietnam. Indeed, one professor of history, Richard Drinnon, in a 1980 book, pointedly charged that Carson and his soldiers in the Navajo campaign were "forerunners of the Burning Fifth Marines" with their Zippo lighters and flamethrowers. And he added that whether burning hogans or hootches, both groups, though separated by more than a century, were arsonists with common attitudes and assumptions.[1]

That slant on history, widely held by intellectuals, writers, and student activists, was quickly communicated to Indians. The Navajo were among the first to seize upon it and to turn the Carson campaign of 1863–1864 to contemporary uses. Thelma S. Guild, co-author with Harvey L. Carter of the most recent Carson biography, visited the Kit Carson Cave near Church Rock, New Mexico, which had been recently vandalized in 1979. When she asked Indians at the trading post about it, one replied angrily, "No one here will talk about Kit Carson. He was a butcher."[2]

Guild observed that "hatred of Carson remains strong among the Navajos."[3] She evidently assumed, as do many others, that such fierce animosity stems directly from tribal traditions and recollections of the Navajos' defeat by Kit in the 1860s. It is fairly easy to document, however, that such is not the case. Carson baiting on the Navajo Reservation was not in evidence much before 1970, when it became a learned behavior, one apparently acquired from non-Indian activists. In the 1950s, one could travel the huge reservation and scarcely find any resident who had ever heard of Kit Carson, as is confirmed by reference to Navajo memoirs of the defeat, collected from participants or their children and translated into English and published by the tribe itself prior to 1970. Given the circumstances, the chronicles can be conceded a degree of reliability. That is, they are as close to the original Indian view as we are likely to get.

A quick reading of these recollections prompts two interesting observations. The first thing one notices is how small an impression Kit Carson made on the Navajo during the war; his name is mentioned seldom and only in passing. Usually, the attacks by Utes, Apaches, and Pueblos, who ganged up on the Navajo as the army made its sweep, receive much more attention in the native accounts. Clearly, in the minds of Navajos who were on the scene in the 1860s, Carson was not regarded as the hated butcher that reservation residents of the 1970s imagined. In any case, as scholar Ruth M. Underhill so aptly pointed out, "Kit Carson killed crops not Navajos."[4]

The second point to be noted in the oral literature is how often informants who lived through that tragic era candidly admit that the Navajo brought disaster upon themselves by their inability to curb their centuries-old habit of raiding their neighbors. Unarguably, that was the central cause of the last great Navajo war, although we have to acknowledge that a wide variety of secondary causes also contributed. Therefore, to heap blame upon Carson and to charge him with chief responsibility for the Navajos' misfortunes, which is the dogma preached today, does both history and the man a grievous disservice.[5]

This is just a single example of how Kit Carson's bad press in the larger society has trickled down to the Indians, coloring their view of him with a tar brush. The earlier oral literature serves as a useful corrective, demolishing the common assumption that modern excoriations of Kit by both academic historians and the media are legitimately derived from authentic tribal traditions. In other words, those who believe that present-day blastings of Kit represent simply a belated recognition of what Indians knew all along are demonstrably dead wrong.

The negative trickle-down, of course, has not been limited to Indians. The fierce twenty-year assault on Kit's good name has left it in tatters among the general public. People speak and write today as if it were an established fact that Kit Carson has been convicted of maniacal crimes against history.

The following quotations, from among the innumerable examples available, handily illustrate how widespread negative views of Carson have become. "Kit Carson was directly or indirectly responsible for the deaths of thousands of Indians," claims a recent and popular picture history of the Old West.[6] A Colorado journalist mentions that Carson "betrayed [the Navajo], starved them by destroying their farms and livestock in Canyon de Chelly, and then brutally marched them to the Bosque Redondo concentration camp."[7] "Kit Carson was a ruthless and brilliant Indian killer," says a distinguished professor in print, as he urges the removal of Kit's name from a mountain in the Sangre de Cristo Range.[8] Taos militants in 1973, while campaigning to change the name of Kit Carson State Park, charged that the town's favorite frontiersman was "a tramp and renegade, liable for the deaths of many Indians."[9]

It is not uncommon for writers to take passing potshots at Carson now that his reputation for evil is firmly in place. In preparing a draft of a new official brochure for the Santa Fe National Historic Trail, researchers at the Harpers Ferry Center of the National Park Service referred to Kit Carson as among the pioneers who "carved their sometimes nefarious names in western lore."[10] Even the *Taos News,* in announcing the 1993 Kit Carson Conference, identified him as "the infamous Taos explorer."[11]

The avalanche of Carson slurs extends, not surprisingly, to our regional literature. New Mexico essayist and short story writer Jim Sagel characterizes Kit as "the famous scout who exploited the Indian people of the Southwest with such success."[12] Popular mystery writer Tony Hillerman declares that Carson National Forest was named for Indian killer Kit Carson.[13] And Taos novelist John Nichols routinely likens Kit to Adolf Hitler.[14] During a 1990 scholarly gathering at Gunnison, Colorado, Nichols sprang up on the stage after a speaker mentioned Carson and, according to press reports, performed an impromptu song he'd scrawled out moments before. In the words of the *Denver Post,* Mr. Nichols "pounded the piano and wailed away with a savagely satiric, boogie-woogie blues ditty about a bloodthirsty, genocidal Carson driving Navajos on their 1860s Long Walk across New Mexico to a concentration camp."[15]

In the contemporary movement to impugn Carson's name, the buzzword "genocide" is frequently linked to Kit, just as it was pinned to Columbus during his quincentenary year. A three-page story on Carson appearing in the *Colorado Springs Gazette Telegraph,* May 16, 1993, began with this statement printed in bold, oversize type: "Kit Carson has become the Christopher Columbus of the West." It was automatically assumed that readers would understand the connection, because both men these days are regularly alleged to have committed genocide against the Indians. The pair of Christophers, in fact, have become trendy new symbols of barbarism.

One of the earliest incidents in which Kit was publicly accused of genocide occurred on the Colorado College campus in the fall of 1972. A new associate professor of anthropology, Dr. Shirley Hill Witt, happened to notice a photograph of Kit Carson hanging in the foyer of the building that housed the R.O.T.C. office. Indignant, she went straight to the college dean and demanded removal of the image, saying that she found it unacceptable. The photograph was promptly taken down. In the brief flurry of publicity that followed, Dr. Witt said this to the media: "I find it perfectly offensive to have a terrorist and killer displayed with honor. The Southwest must be bankrupt for heroes, if it has to enshrine the likes of Kit Carson." And she stigmatized him as "a genocidal racist."[16]

Historian Harvey L. Carter afterward published an article challenging Dr. Witt's assertions and marshaling evidence showing that Kit was anything but a racist and that he never committed genocide. "It is unfortunate that she did not undertake to do some investigation of Carson's life and the considerable literature concerning him," Carter responded mildly.[17] In truth, Dr. Witt gave no indication that she knew anything at all about Carson's biography or that she had made the slightest attempt to get her facts straight.

This episode established a pattern that would become all too common over the next two decades. Whenever anyone needed a scapegoat or whipping boy in speaking of the Old West, Kit Carson was trotted to the fore and exhibited as the model exploiter and murderer who epitomized the true and suppressed history of frontier America. The purveyors of such nonsense could offer no factual support for their claims and were expressing ill-informed opinions rather than sound historical judgments. But the public was usually unable to make that distinction.

People like Hillerman and Nichols — who write voluminously about the Southwest, are celebrity figures, and who associate with other celebrities like Robert Redford — are granted high credibility by our image-conscious society. If they say that Kit Carson was a scoundrel and Indian killer, many innocent persons will swear that it is true. And in the same manner, if a professor with a Ph.D. degree, like Dr. Witt, proclaims that Kit was a genocidal racist, what humble man in the street would dare to contradict?

In almost every case, those making serious accusations against Kit can be shown to have neglected their homework, an inexcusable omission, because the details of his life are available and quite accessible.[18] John Nichols, for instance, in speaking at the Albuquerque Public Library, October 13, 1990, admitted when questioned that he could not give the title of a single book he had ever read on Kit Carson.[19] One might have guessed that, upon hearing him sing his Gunnison "boogie woogie blues ditty," which referred to Kit driving Navajos across New Mexico on the Long Walk. In fact, Kit was at home in Taos, resting on leave, and did not conduct the Indians to their new reservation in Bosque Redondo.

The anti-Carson utterances that are hurled like brickbats these days have nothing to do with the honest promotion of history. Rather, they are meant, in the nature of propaganda, to support particular social or political agendas, wherein the ends justify the means, and the past can be manipulated to achieve some lofty contemporary goal.[20] Before explaining further how that situation influences the public perception of Carson, I will turn to the historical record in an attempt to accurately assess Kit's behavior and attitudes toward Indians in general and then will examine what happened to the historical record as it succumbed to distortion over the past century.

To determine what Kit Carson thought about Indians, and to describe with some accuracy his treatment of them, we need to review three things. The first is what Kit himself said on the subject. But inasmuch as people frequently say one thing and then do another, it is necessary to compare Kit's statements with his actions — a simple task because his biography is fairly complete. Finally, in trying to plumb the matter, we can go to Carson's contemporaries, to persons who knew him, both Indian and white, and observe what they had to say. Although most people are apt to harbor some bias, that can be controlled by following the common threads that run through the majority of testimonies.

Kit grew up on the family farm in hostile Indian country in central Missouri. When war parties moved through the area and the alarm was raised, the Carsons and their neighbors fled to the security of nearby Fort Hempstead, a pioneer stockade. In 1813, Kit's father, Lindsey Carson, was wounded while pursuing Sac and Iowa raiders.[21] Long afterward, Mary Ann Carson, a younger sister of Kit, said, "Indians were a constant peril in those days, and we always were afraid of them."[22] She qualified this statement, however, by asserting that Kit had no fear, and when peaceful parties passed by, he would approach them with curiosity and a show of friendliness. If that was actually the case, it might indicate an early affinity for Indians, which was not that rare among frontier youth.

Carson's most recent biographers, on the other hand, suggest that, based on his early experiences, he probably absorbed the typical attitude of the day toward Indians: "They were different and not to be trusted."[23] Or, if Richard Drinnon is right that Indian-hating was rooted in fears and prejudices buried deep in the Western psyche, then the boy Kit must have been afflicted with that inherent racism that is now so often claimed for the entire white pioneer class.[24]

In truth, there is no direct evidence to support such a view; in fact, solid grounds exist for believing that Kit's friendly but realistic appraisal of Indians was acquired during his formative years in Missouri and further refined during his trapper period. In 1826, at age sixteen, he ran away to New Mexico. After some bouncing around, he gravitated to Taos, where he fell under the influence of seasoned mountain man Ewing Young. Having trapped the Southwest and fought Indians since the early 1820s, Young was "one of the best teachers the fur trade could supply," and over the next several years he taught his pupil, the green Missouri boy, well.[25]

In the summer of 1829, Young left Taos with a party of forty men on a trapping expedition that would take them in the next twenty months through the beaver country of southern Arizona and then on up California's San Joaquin Valley to the Sacramento Valley. Kit Carson joined as an apprentice mountaineer (as mountain men were usually called in that era), and on this excursion he got his first serious lessons in dealing with the Indians of the Far West.

Ewing Young and men like him had already adopted some basic rules of conduct that were shaped by their observations and experiences in the wilds. Their first law of survival was: never let an affront by Indians go unpunished. Any sign of weakness or hesitation could prove fatal, because it invited further attack. On the other hand, as they well knew, virtually all tribes respected strength, courage, force, and success. From necessity then, the trappers adhered firmly to the principle of retaliation.

That was the practical side of the equation, but there was also an emotional side, which became evident when the roaming white men suffered casualties. As Kit's friend John C. Frémont once put it, upon losing his mountaineer guide to an Indian arrow: "Men who have gone through such dangers and sufferings as we had seen, become like brothers, and feel each other's loss. To defend and avenge each other is the deep feeling of all." [26] And mountain man "Uncle Dick" Wootton reiterated that sentiment in his memoirs, recalling that "Our friendships were warm . . . and it was seldom indeed that the killing or wounding of one of our number had gone unavenged."[27]

The desire for retribution was just as strong among most Indian groups. The Plains tribes, for instance, habitually raided their enemies for horses and booty. And upon suffering similar raids, they would organize revenge parties. Such ceaseless rounds of attacks and counterattacks allowed Indian males to achieve advancement and status through war exploits.[28]

James Kaywaykla, an Apache of the Southwest who lived through the final wars with the white men, told an interviewer in the 1950s that it was their "obligation" to retaliate for the wrongs inflicted upon them and that they were "taught that revenge is obligatory."[29] One of his fellow tribesmen, Asa Daklugie, phrased it even more succinctly: "Revenge was part of our philosophy."[30] Because raiding was one of the chief industries of Apache men, an activity that invited reprisals from their victims, the tribe was perpetually spoiling for revenge against someone.

As the principle of retaliation was almost universal among native peoples of the West, its ready assimilation by the trappers is scarcely surprising. As a class they willingly absorbed Indian speech, costume, and modes of conduct and frequently took Indian wives, because it facilitated their life in the wilderness but also because they preferred it that way.[31] The revenge factor, therefore, provides a key to understanding the behavior of both Indians and whites and, thus, the conduct of Kit Carson, who saw the principle vividly applied during his first trapping venture under Ewing Young.

In 1826, Young had led another band of fur hunters into southern Arizona and near the confluence of the Salt and Gila Rivers encountered three wretched men, the only survivors of a large party of French-American trappers ambushed by Papagos. As one of the participants wrote long afterward, Young's mountaineers went after the Indians for "purposes of vengeance." They completely vanquished the village and recovered and buried the mutilated bodies of the dead trappers.[32] The episode conformed perfectly to the "philosophy" of retaliation.

Kit would have learned all about retaliation when he set forth with Ewing Young in 1829 and would have heard too how another party sent by Young to Arizona the previous year had been badly mauled by the Apaches. Hence, their agenda included not only trapping but also one more exercise in retribution. In his autobiography, Carson describes how the hostile Apaches were lured into a trap and were routed, losing fifteen or twenty warriors.[33] His education in frontier realities had begun.

There was a supplement, like a codicil, to the principle of retaliation that lent even more ominous overtones. Joseph R. Walker, a mountain man whom Kit came to know in the years following the Young expedition, defined the supplement neatly in a chance remark. He said, "Under Indian law when one [member] of a tribe offends, the whole tribe is responsible."[34] That was a convenient idea, because the identity of individual raiders or thieves was usually impossible to establish, but it was not difficult to identify the tribe to which they belonged. The white man in general, and mountaineers in particular, took the same view. In the face of perceived wrongs by others, most people will resort to retaliation if the opportunity presents itself and will assign guilt collectively, rather than individually. While leading a small wagon train over the Santa Fe Trail toward New Mexico in 1851, Carson very nearly fell victim to the codicil.

In western Kansas he ran across a band of Cheyenne, whom he assumed were friendly, and so, in sign language, he invited them to sit down for a smoke and talk. The Indians did not know that Kit understood the Cheyenne tongue, and he soon learned through their unguarded exchanges that they planned to kill him and his men. Their justification lay with a party of soldiers that had passed ten days ahead of the Carson caravan. The officer in charge had seized the Cheyenne chief for some petty indiscretion and had flogged him. "An Indian very seldom lets an injury go unavenged, and it is immaterial who his victim may be, so long as he belongs to the same nation as the offender. Unfortunately, I happened to be the first American to pass them since the insult was given, and on me they proposed to retaliate." [35] That was Kit's assessment of the situation.

When he informed the surprised Cheyenne that he was aware of their hostile intentions, they withdrew, but only a short distance, making it plain that they would return in their own time and destroy the wagon train. Under cover of darkness, Carson sped a messenger up the trail toward Rayado, New Mexico, to summon aid. When Cheyenne warriors reappeared the next day, he told them that friends would soon be coming to his aid. He also explained that if he were killed, his friends would know by whom it was done, and he guaranteed them: "my death would be avenged." [36] That was exactly the sort of talk Indians understood. Therefore, the war party, after pondering his words, rode away and left Kit Carson alone.

Even when all parties know that the principle of retaliation allows reprisals upon the innocent, persons who suffer because someone else in their racial or ethnic group has committed violent acts are quite likely to raise a protest and denounce the unfairness of it all. Even Kit, momentarily at least, gave way to that natural inclination when he first heard the Cheyenne say they wanted to slay him. As he recalled: "I told the Indians that I was ignorant of the cause of their wishing my scalp, and that I had done them no injury and wanted to treat them kindly." [37]

His statement is reminiscent of one made by Navajo leader Manuelito in 1864 after the army defeated his tribe and was preparing to remove it to the new reservation on the Pecos River. Speaking for his own immediate band, Manuelito asked: "Why must we go to the Bosque? We have never stolen or murdered, and have at all times kept the peace we promised General Canby."[38] The answer, as the chief well knew, was that the Navajo were being condemned to exile collectively — the entire tribe held responsible for the transgressions of a few.

A twentieth-century Navajo, Dugal Tsosie Begay, remembered his grandfather telling him that "it was our own fault that we were rounded up and taken to Fort Sumner [Bosque Redondo]. They said we used to kill Ute Indians, Pueblo Indians, and Mexicans and bring their sheep back, and that these actions caused the wars between us, the Army, and other Indian tribes."[39] Here was conscious acknowledgment of the retaliation principle.

Against this background, we can begin to understand Kit Carson's true attitude and behavior toward Indians. Like the natives who inhabited the mountain West, he and his fellow trappers recognized the revenge factor and, moreover, adhered to the common notion that the entire tribe was responsible for the conduct of individual members. Those are fundamental keys to explaining what happened on the frontier.

As long ago as 1968, Harvey L. Carter, in his justly celebrated book, *Dear Old Kit,* explained all this and pointed out that Carson "fought Indians on a retaliatory principle, but he did so in the belief that this was necessary in order to ensure the safety of white men traveling in the Indian country."[40] He added that the motive for his fighting was not only retributory but also defensive and, occasionally, preventative in nature.

The historical evidence overwhelmingly supports Carter's judgment. In Kit's memoirs, which he dictated in 1856, he mentions some twenty-five hostile encounters with Indians that he had experienced to that date. That figure grew during the last decade of his life when he led major military campaigns against the Mescalero Apache, Navajo, Comanche, and Kiowa. The latter episodes, in particular, are fully documented, and indications are that Carson conducted himself properly while engaged in a declared war and acted in most cases with commendable restraint.

General James F. Rusling, who met Kit at Fort Garland, Colorado, in 1867, claimed that no American knew Indians better than Carson, nor did the Indians have a stouter friend than he.[41] During his tenure as Indian agent in the late 1850s, Kit repeatedly warned that the tribes needed to be protected from unscrupulous Americans and native New Mexicans who stole from them and traded them whiskey, because those crimes always led to trouble. "The Indians know no law but retaliation," he pointed out sagely.[42]

Even from this brief summary, it ought to be clear how Kit Carson regarded Indians and what his motives were when he fought them. On the charges of genocide and racism, the historical record clearly exonerates him. The accusation of genocide, which did not even surface until the last half of the twentieth century, is patently untrue. And as for Kit's alleged racism, that bit of silliness can only be indulged in by people who know nothing of his personal life. After all, the man's first two wives were Indians, his third wife was Hispanic, all of his children were ethnically mixed, he adopted a

Navajo boy (naming him Juan Carson), and the language spoken in his Taos home for twenty-five years was Spanish.

For his day, Kit Carson was about as tolerant as they came. The plain fact is that he was a man of character in an age when character still counted. If Thomas Jefferson was right that a natural aristocracy existed among men, grounded in virtue, talents, and merit, then Carson unquestionably qualified for membership.[43] By no stretch of the imagination can he legitimately be cast as a frontier villain. And it can be proven that the Kit Carson today depicted as a racist, Indian hater, and wanton killer is an invented myth.

The chain of circumstances that led to creation of that myth is long and complicated and can only be summarized here. What we need to remember is that the campaign to malign Kit Carson's name is not accidental or haphazard, for there is method and purpose in evidence. It is probably not too far afield to claim that Kit's troubles, as regards his reputation, originated with the dime novels, a genre of trashy literature popular in the nineteenth century. Authors of these thin publications borrowed the names of famous westerners and around them fabricated dramatic tales filled with blood and gore. Produced for mass circulation, the dime novels preyed upon the gullibility of the reading public, which seemed unable to distinguish between fact and fiction.

An early example of this type appeared in 1849: Charles E. Averill's *Kit Carson: The Prince of the Gold Hunters*.[44] Other titles soon followed. In them, Kit was transformed into a hero of countless violent exploits. Most of his antagonists were Indians, and he was represented as fearlessly slaying them by the dozens. Fed a steady dose of such stories, the public in time came to believe that engaging in slaughter constituted Carson's main activity in life.

The exploitation of his name by the dime novelists set Kit's teeth on edge, but there was little at the time that he could do about it. When a journalist for the *Washington Union* asked him whether the Averill story was true, he replied that every statement made about him was false.[45] On another occasion, when someone handed him a copy of the book, he vigorously expressed his disgust and threatened to "burn the damn thing."[46] The image of Indian slayer, despite its untruthfulness, thereafter would stick to his heels like glue.

Colonel John M. Chivington, who led the massacre of Cheyenne at Sand Creek, Colorado, in 1864, was apparently one of those influenced by the fictional literature. In all likelihood, his reading of dime novels about Kit led him to remark shortly after his bloody episode: "I have eclipsed . . . Carson, and posterity will speak of me as the great Indian fighter."[47] In fact, both posterity and Kit completely repudiated him, and the latter referred to him as "that dog Chivington."[48]

Even though some fairly solid historical works covering Carson's life existed alongside the dime novels, it was this fictional dross that impressed itself upon the popular mind.[49] One category of readers who made unprincipled use of this worthless material was composed of people whom Harvey L. Carter has termed "pseudo-companions of Carson."[50] They were old men who, during the early twentieth century, attracted attention to themselves by wearing buckskins and by claiming to have been closely associated with Kit in his early trapping days. Of the lot, the best known were Oliver Perry Wiggins, Captain William Drannon, and Colonel Dick Rutledge. Such individuals, in their own writings or in press interviews, spun fanciful yarns about Carson's wild adventures and bloody Indian fights. For inspiration, story lines, and detail it is evident that they drew liberally from the dime novel literature. In many quarters, these bold impostors were taken at face value (Wiggins was not exposed as a fraud until the 1960s), and hence their narratives appeared, at least to the historically naive, to reinforce the dime novel image of Kit as an efficient exterminator of Indians.[51]

Reference to two acts of vandalism, that occurred almost ninety years apart, will illustrate what can happen when individuals fall under the spell of the fictionalized Kit Carson.

The first incident took place in the Colorado State Capitol building during the summer of 1903. High up in the dome are sixteen stained glass portraits of pioneers listed in the state's Hall of Fame. Among those immortalized in glass was Kit Carson.[52] On July 16 the capitol janitor, Pat Boyle, heard a pounding noise in the dome and, looking up, saw a man leaning over the balcony swinging a large stone on the end of a rope against the Carson portrait below him. When Boyle yelled for him to stop, the man laughed wildly. The janitor dashed up the spiral stairs to the balcony and, upon reaching it, observed two men wrestling the vandal to the floor. They admitted to being his friends and identified him as Josiah S. Winthrop of Bingham, Massachusetts. Winthrop, they said, had become demented owing to Denver's high altitude and to his excessive reading and studying about Indians. He belonged to a New England association called The Society for the Betterment of the Red Man, and his attack upon the Carson glass was because he opposed honoring a man who had killed off "poor Lo" in large numbers. The men stated that Winthrop had visited the capitol earlier and, seeing Kit's portrait, had been planning ever since to destroy it. The glass portrait had to be completely replaced.[53] The widely accepted fiction that Kit Carson was a spectacular Indian killer had been powerful enough to precipitate Winthrop's violent criminal act.

In a similar manner, vandals in late August 1990 must have heard once too often that Kit Carson was the equal of Adolf Hitler, for in the darkness of night they assaulted his gravesite in the Taos cemetery, spray painted swastikas and the word "Nazi" on the monuments of Kit and his wife Josepha, and defaced a historical plaque.[54]

How is it possible to explain the stubborn persistence of a Carson image molded in the shape of a monstrous Indian slayer when the obvious and rather simple facts of his life point to no such thing? The answer in part can be found in the old truism: Myths will not yield to facts. Once a myth has taken hold in the popular mind, no amount of empirical evidence is likely to overthrow it. Because Americans have long held that the voice of the people is the voice of truth, once a fantasy or myth becomes accepted in the street, it receives automatic validation. This notion of the people's infallibility runs early and deep through American history, although it seemed to crystallize with the ascent of the common man to power upon the election of President Andrew Jackson in 1828. In the following decade, foreign observers first began to note this peculiarly American phenomenon — the tyranny of public opinion.

That tyranny reached its apogee in the last decades of the twentieth century, when public opinion polls became a standard measure for ascertaining truths. In the "everyone knows" approach to history, when Kit Carson became recognized as a genocidal racist and a petty Adolf Hitler, those depictions passed from the realm of opinion to the realm of established dogma. In the process, the niceties of evidence, based on historical fact, were conveniently ignored.

Contemporary British historian Paul Johnson has remarked that one of the most puzzling features of the modern mind is its aversion to facts, an attitude that leads to moral anarchy.[55] Those who so breezily label Kit a racist and a Hitler, without offering evidence, and who feel no guilt or remorse in doing so, illustrate his point. In the postmodern world, fact has been superseded by theory and by popular consensus, reason has been abandoned as unreliable, and reality is regarded as a mirage. In such a climate, the transmutation of Kit Carson from a nineteenth-century hero into a twentieth-century villain is easily achieved.

Still, it seems legitimate to demand that Carson's detractors be required to lay something in the way of traditional evidence upon the table to support their serious charges and to make it available for public review. Thus far, his critics have generally been unwilling to take that step, perhaps having forgotten that the first rule of history is to tell the truth. They also need to be reminded that facts count, that evidence matters, and that public opinion is not a reliable source of information. Only if those fundamentals are observed can Kit Carson's reputation be fairly judged.

History Professor Anne M. Butler of Utah State University mentions in a recent article that at a professional meeting she was denounced by a fellow historian after she had made a presentation. According to her, "In a blistering fit of rage, [he] screamed at me that I was part of the 'Kit Carson' approach to history. He wasn't trying to be witty."[56] I don't know what traditionalist views Dr. Butler might have expressed to provoke such an outburst, but it is a stunning oddity that Kit's name has become not only an epithet but also a synonym for supposedly "reactionary" thought.

So deep-seated is the current belief that Kit Carson was an Indian hater and brutal assassin that anyone who attempts to marshal the facts and prove otherwise is apt to be stigmatized as an apologist or accused of being defensive. Dr. Patricia Nelson Limerick, a leading New Western Historian, was quoted by a journalist who asked her to give an opinion on the 1993 Kit Carson Conference. She replied: "I think Kit Carson would be very angry that these wimpy intellectuals feel it necessary to be defending him."[57] The remark, if accurately recorded, reveals a complete lack of understanding of both Carson and of the forces at work undermining his reputation. But in its deficiencies, the observation is quite contemporary.

Like all men everywhere, Kit Carson had his faults and personal flaws; otherwise, he would have been a saint rather than a homespun American frontiersman. But unlike most of his companions, his many outstanding character traits far outweighed his deficiencies. He was neither bloodthirsty, mean-spirited, cowardly, nor irresponsible. On the contrary, in the words of Albert Richardson, who knew him personally in the 1850s, Kit was "a gentleman by instinct, upright, pure, and simple-hearted, beloved alike by Indians, Mexicans, and Americans."[58] Plenty of others, who were in a position to know, seconded that praise.

"Ultimately, everything depends on the quality of the individual," psychologist Carl Jung once wrote.[59] If that is the case, and there seems little reason to doubt it, then Kit Carson ought to be recognized for his honorable career in settling the West and for his performance as a man of quality. At the same time, the groundless accusations that he hated Indians and delighted in killing them ought to be put to rest, once and for all.

NOTES

1. Richard Drinnon, *Facing West: The Metaphysics of Indian-Hating and Empire Building* (Minneapolis: University of Minnesota Press, 1980), p. 459. See also a news statement in the *Denver Post*, November 4, 1973: "Many Indians, especially the Navajos, see little difference between Carson's treatment of their ancestors and the massacre at My Lai."
2. Thelma S. Guild and Harvey L. Carter, *Kit Carson: A Pattern for Heroes* (Lincoln: University of Nebraska Press, 1984), p. 330, n. 55.
3. Guild and Carter, *Kit Carson*, p. 330, n. 55.
4. Ruth M. Underhill, *The Navajos* (Norman: University of Oklahoma Press, 1956), p. 118.
5. See the observations of Friday Kinlicheenee in Broderick H. Johnson, ed., *Navajo Stories of the Long Walk Period* (Tsaile, Ariz.: Navajo Community College Press, 1973), p. 238. Navajo medicine man Frank Mitchell was among those who acknowledged that his tribe's raiding was the main cause of their woes. Charlotte Frisbie and David P. McAllester, eds., *Navajo Blessingway Singer: The Autobiography of Frank Mitchell, 1881–1967* (Tucson: University of Arizona Press, 1980), p. 17.

    A recent book by Tiana Bighorse, *Bighorse the Warrior* (Tucson: University of Arizona Press, 1990) contains several anti-Carson statements by a Navajo. Supposedly, they express the sentiments of the author's father, who lived through the Navajo campaign and died in 1939. Ms. Bighorse, however, did not record her recollections of her father's stories until the 1970s, at the height of the anti-Kit crusade, so one has to wonder if she did not, perhaps unconsciously, absorb the propaganda of her day and project it backward as fact. See, for instance, the remark about Kit on p. 28, which seems to have a very contemporary, non Indian ring to it. On the other hand, Ms. Bighorse could possibly be one of those rare individuals whose historical memory contains more fact than fiction, so that her Carson reference may indeed be an accurate reflection of her late father's views.
6. Virginia Hopkins, *Pioneers of the Old West* (New York: Bonanza Books, 1988), p. 40.
7. From Ed Quillen's column in the *Denver Post*, April 27, 1993.
8. Devon Peña, "Townhouse 14," *La Tertulia* [Colorado College], 4:2 (Spring 1988): 2.
9. *Denver Post*, November 4, 1973.
10. In reviewing the draft of the brochure, I urged the National Park Service to delete the unwarranted and gratuitous word "nefarious" from the final version.
11. *Taos News*, March 18, 1993.

12. The line appears in Jim Sagel, *The Holy Cheese* (Hanover, N.H.: Ediciones del Norte, 1990), p. 125.
13. Tony Hillerman, "First Americans Lack First Amendment's Religious Protection," *Book Talk* [Newsletter of the New Mexico Book League], 22:2 (April 1993): 2. See also the anti-Carson statements of one of his fictional Navajo characters in *Coyote Waits* (New York: Harper & Row, 1990), p. 170.
14. As an example, see John Nichols, "Can a Yuppie Marxist Really Find Happiness in the Land of Entrapment?" *El Palacio,* 97:2 (Spring/Summer 1991): 51. Harry Walters, director of the historical and cultural museum at Navajo Community College in Tsaile, Arizona, was recently quoted as saying that defending Kit Carson "is like trying to rehabilitate Adolf Hitler." *Santa Fe Reporter,* June 30, 1993.
15. *Denver Post,* October 7, 1990.
16. Harvey L. Carter, "The Curious Case of the Slandered Scout, the Aggressive Anthropologist, the Delinquent Dean, and the Acquiescent Army," *Denver Westerner's Brand Book* (Boulder, Colo.: The Westerners, 1973): 95, 98.
17. Ibid., p. 107.
18. Among authoritative works are: Harvey L. Carter, *Dear Old Kit: The Historical Christopher Carson* (Norman: University of Oklahoma Press, 1968); Thelma S. Guild and Harvey L. Carter, *Kit Carson: A Pattern for Heroes* (Lincoln: University of Nebraska Press, 1984); M. Morgan Estergreen, *Kit Carson: A Portrait in Courage* (Norman: University of Oklahoma Press, 1962); Milo M. Quaife, ed., *Kit Carson's Autobiography* (Chicago. The Lakeside Press, 1935).
19. I was present on that occasion and posed the question.
20. Dr. Witt, for example, used her college office as the regional headquarters for the militant American Indian Movement, of which she was an officer, although a non-Indian herself. That membership, one suspects, explains her shrill and inaccurate attacks upon Kit Carson.
21. *The Metropolitan* [Jefferson City, Missouri], November 9, 1847.
22. Estergreen, *Kit Carson,* p. 19.
23. Guild and Carter, *Kit Carson,* p. 8.
24. *Facing West,* p. 463. The author, Drinnon, presaged the New Western Historians of the late 1980s, who concluded, in the words of Patricia Nelson Limerick, that "Race . . . was the key factor in dividing the people of Western America." *Legacy of Conquest* (New York: W. W. Norton, 1987), p. 280.
25. Kenneth L. Holmes, *Ewing Young: Master Trapper* (Portland, Oreg.: Binfords & Mort, 1967), p. 57.
26. George Douglas Brewerton, *Overland with Kit Carson* (New York: A. L. Burt Company, 1930), p. 96.
27. Howard Louis Conard, *"Uncle Dick" Wootton* (Chicago: W. E. Dibble & Company, 1890), pp. 178–179.
28. Bernard Mishkin, *Rank and Warfare Among the Plains Indians* (Seattle: University of Washington Press, 1966), p. 1.
29. Eve Ball, *In the Days of Victorio* (Tucson: University of Arizona Press, 1970), pp. 119–120.
30. Eve Ball, *Indeh: An Apache Odyssey* (Provo, Utah: Brigham Young University Press, 1980), p. 58.

31. Henry Nash Smith, *Virgin Land: The American West as Symbol and Myth* (New York: Vintage Books, 1950), p. 88.
32. Charles L. Camp, ed., *George C. Yount and His Chronicles of the West* (Denver: Old West Publishing Co., 1966), pp. 32–33.
33. Quaife, *Kit Carson's Autobiography,* p. 10.
34. Bil Gilbert, *Westering Man: The Life of Joseph Walker* (New York: Atheneum, 1983), p. 159.
35. Quaife, *Kit Carson's Autobiography,* p. 142.
36. Ibid., p. 144.
37. Ibid., p. 143.
38. Quoted in Dee Brown, *Bury My Heart at Wounded Knee* (New York: Holt, Rinehart, 1971), p. 29.
39. Johnson, *Navajo Stories of the Long Walk Period,* p. 213.
40. *Dear Old Kit,* p. 197. On the same subject, see Carter, "The Slandered Scout," p. 101.
41. James F. Rusling, *Across America; or The Great West* (New York: Sheldon and Company, 1875), pp. 137–138.
42. Kit Carson to Indian Superintendent James L. Collins, Taos, June 24, 1857, BIA, Superintendency of New Mexico, 1849–1880, National Archives, Reel 1. In 1865, Carson testified that age-old feuds among the tribes themselves were based mainly on "long cherished traditions of delayed revenge." See his letter written from Fort Lyon, Colorado, to Capt. B. C. Cutler, August 19, 1865, in *Condition of the Indian Tribes* (Washington: GPO, 1867), pp. 438–440.
43. Jefferson is quoted in Louis B. Wright and H. T. Swendenberg, Jr., eds., *The American Tradition* (New York: F. S. Crofts and Company, 1941), p. 44.
44. Richard Slotkin, *The Fatal Environment: The Myth of the Frontier in the Age of Industrialization, 1800–1890* (New York: Atheneum, 1985), p. 202. The term "dime novel" properly dated from 1860, but publications using the same formula and with an inexpensive price had been available at least two decades earlier.
45. *The Washington Union,* August 29, 1857.
46. *The Colorado Sun,* August 23, 1879. (Clipping from the Dawson Scrapbooks, vol. 1, Colorado Historical Society, Denver.)
47. Quoted in Lonnie J. White, ed., *Chronicle of a Congressional Journey: The Doolittle Committee in the Southwest, 1865* (Boulder, Colo.: Pruett Publishing Company, 1975), p. 27.
48. Rusling, *Across America,* p. 138.
49. See especially the first Carson biography, De Witt C. Peters, *The Life of Kit Carson, the Nestor of the Rockies* (New York: W.R.C. Clark & Company, 1858); and Donald Jackson and Mary Lee Spence, eds., *The Expeditions of John Charles Frémont, 1838–1844* (Urbana: University of Illinois Press, 1970).
50. His use of the phrase appears in *Dear Old Kit,* p. 247. For his examples, see pp. 18–23.
51. For an excellent treatment of Wiggins, see Lorene and Kenneth Englert, *Oliver Perry Wiggins, Fantastic, Bombastic Frontiersman* (Palmer Lake, Colo: Filter Press, 1968).
52. Mary and Gene Martin, *Colorado's Hall of Fame* (Colorado Springs, Colo.: Little London Press, 1974), pp. 10–11.
53. A full account is given in the *Denver Republican,* July 17, 1903. (Clipping form the Dawson Scrapbooks, vol. 1, Colorado Historical Society, Denver.) On replacing the damaged

Carson portrait, see undated clipping ca. August 17, 1903, in the Kit Carson File, Pioneers Museum, Colorado Springs.

54. *The Taos News,* August 30, 1990.
55. Paul Johnson, *Modern Times: The World from the Twenties to the Eighties* (New York: Harper Colophon Books, 1983), pp. 10–11. Also see the review of his book in *The American Spectator,* 17 (August 1984), p. 21.
56. Anne M. Butler, "Laugh and the West Might Laugh With You," *Journal of the West,* 32 (April 1993), p. 4.
57. *Santa Fe Reporter,* June 30, 1993. The quote was taken in a telephone interview, June 23, 1993, by journalist Josh Kurtz, who — upon checking his notes at my request — confirmed its accuracy.
58. Albert Richardson, *Beyond the Mississippi* (Hartford, Conn.: American Publishing Company, 1867), p. 261.
59. C. G. Jung, *The Undiscovered Self* (New York: American Library, 1958), p. 67.

CHAPTER 5

An Indian Before Breakfast: Kit Carson Then and Now

Robert M. Utley

Did Kit Carson really revel in killing an Indian before breakfast? Or was he the Carson of my youth — "dear old Kit," "the happy warrior?"

Maybe both, probably neither. But I offer this essay not to explore which or neither but with a plea that Kit Carson be allowed to live in his own world rather than in yours and mine. Carson is one of those figures out of the past who tells more about the generation looking at him than about who he really was. General Custer is another. So, as we have recently seen, is Columbus. Such figures are mirrors reflecting the beliefs and aspirations of the beholders rather than the true character of the beholden. As the beholders change, so do the beholden. And so one generation's happy warrior is transformed into another generation's bloodthirsty butcher.

This is what the historical profession calls "presentism" — the impulse to judge people and events of the past according to the values and standards of today. What Kit Carson did to the Navajos in 1863–1864 does not fit today's conception of humanity. But Carson knew nothing of today's conception of humanity. He marched to an altogether different drummer. He was a product of his time and place, not our time and place. Should he not be judged, or at least understood, as an inhabitant of that world rather than this one?

I have always believed that the historian bears an obligation to judge both. A true understanding of what people of the past did and why can only be reached by looking at them within the cultural and historical milieu in which they existed. Yet history is timely and relevant only when laid against a backdrop of modern norms. The latter, however, should be implicit, not a polemic that overwhelms the former.

In looking back on Kit Carson, I exempt the Navajos from this commandment, just as I exempt the Nez Perce for the flight of Chief Joseph and the Lakota for Wounded Knee. Their tribal memory is profoundly personal, for the victims were their forebears. Moreover, the passion of the tribal memory is itself a significant strand of history. However much contradicted by the documentary record, it powerfully bespeaks the intensity of the experience and its historical consequence.

First we need to understand Carson himself. He was not the typical one-dimensional mountain man, a boisterous, hard-drinking, hard-fighting roughneck, who knew how to survive in the mountains but little more. As an acquaintance observed, "There was nothing like the fire-eater in his manners, but, to the contrary, in all his actions he was quiet and unassuming."[1] Although unlettered, he did not lack intellect. His experiences as mountain man, trapper, trader, explorer, guide, Indian fighter, Indian agent, and finally soldier equipped him with many perspectives from which to view life. Thoughtful, conversant in English, Spanish, several Indian dialects, and sign language, he exhibited a depth of thought born of wilderness adventure and a variety of human relationships extraordinary for his time and place.

Wilderness adventure framed Carson's outlook toward Indians. Merely to have survived thirty years in a wilderness inhabited mainly by Indians testified to his understanding of these people and the conditions they imposed on life. He dealt with them successfully both as friends and as enemies. As trapper and guide his rifle brought down uncounted warriors, and he gained renown as an Indian fighter. But he also took two Indian women as wives and formed associations of trust and respect with Indians who showed their friendship. Unlike many of his peers, Carson saw Indians as human beings, to be treated as friends if they gave evidence of friendship, to be treated as enemies if they gave evidence of hostility.

No period of Carson's life better conveys his attitude toward Indians than his incumbency as U.S. Indian agent for the Utes, from 1854 to 1861, with headquarters in Taos, New Mexico. During the early years of his term, both the Utes and the Jicarilla Apaches were at war with the whites, and Carson served frequently as scout and guide for military columns. In these operations he fully lived up to his reputation as premier Indian fighter. When peace was restored, however, Carson treated the Utes with kindness, consideration, and sympathy. He was a much better agent than most produced by the spoils system. He was conscientious, honest, and truthful; he knew the language, thought, and customs of his charges; he listened attentively to their problems; and he reasoned and counseled with them. In return, they accorded him trust and affection.

In commentary dictated while he was the Indian agent, Carson revealed a key to his thinking about Indians. "I frequently visit the Indians," he wrote, "speak to them of the advantages of peace, and use my influence with them to keep them satisfied with the proceedings of those placed in power over them."[2] As he showed most notably in relations with John C. Frémont and James H. Carleton, Carson greatly respected authority. In Indian affairs, he subscribed to the guiding precepts of government policy. Keeping the Utes "satisfied with the proceedings of those placed in power over them" would have been a central purpose of his administration.

Those "proceedings" sprang from two tenets that characterized public sentiment and official policy. Carson subscribed to both.

The first was the right of white pioneers to claim any lands not being occupied and exploited in the approved Anglo–Saxon fashion. In its most florid formulation, this was the doctrine of "manifest destiny," which held that Americans' destiny was manifestly to overspread the continent and, as divinely enjoined by the Creator, make it blossom with the fruits of their labor. Most Indians did not live in permanent dwellings, till the soil, or indeed even look on land as something that could be "owned." The whites believed that Indians must make way, therefore, for settlers capable of drawing from the land all that it could yield. This was an imperious rationalization of American acquisitiveness, of course, but it must also be seen as an honest conviction held by most people of the time.

That Kit Carson bought this notion, or at least did not challenge it, may be glimpsed in his official report of the military operations against the Mescalero Apaches of southern New Mexico. "There no longer exists any reason," he wrote in January 1863, "why the prolific valleys of the Bonito, Pecos and their tributaries should remain uncultivated and the resources of this section of the country . . . remain undeveloped."[3]

The second tenet, which became the keystone of U.S. Indian policy, was that the solution to the Indian problem lay in confining Indian groups to reservations and there teaching them to support themselves by farming. Kit Carson firmly believed in this formula. Time and again as agent, he urged that the government settle the Utes on a reservation as distant as possible from white settlements and help them to become farmers. A nearby military fort would protect them from unwanted whites and unfriendly Indians.[4] This is almost exactly the formula that General Carleton attempted with the Bosque Redondo, with such tragic consequences for the Navajos. That Carson applauded this scheme reflecting his own long-held belief should come as no surprise.

Crucial to an understanding of the Navajo War of 1863–1864 is the climate of mutual fear and hostility that had plagued relations between Navajos and New Mexicans for generations — first under Spain, then Mexico, and most recently the United States. Navajos had robbed, terrorized, enslaved, and butchered New Mexicans. On a lesser scale, New Mexicans had robbed, terrorized, enslaved, and butchered Navajos. New Mexicans supplied arms and ammunition to Navajos, who used them in slaughtering other New Mexicans and paid for them with the proceeds gained in the process. The pattern was fixed by more than a century of practice, and it was not easily broken by either party.[5]

Complicating and aggravating the problem was the Navajos' highly decentralized and democratic political organization. The Indian raids were mostly the work of a few outlaws — *ladrones* — not sanctioned by the propertied elements who made up the tribal power structure — *ricos*. The chiefs, however, could not control the *ladrones*, a reality of Navajo life that escaped the Americans, who insisted on holding the chiefs responsible for the behavior of all the Navajos.

New Mexican retaliation, moreover, usually fell on the peacefully disposed *ricos*, whose abundance of material possessions not only made them more profitable targets but also, because their possessions advertised their whereabouts and hampered their mobility, made them more convenient targets as well. Progressive impoverishment transformed *ricos* into *ladrones*, causing the Navajo peace party to shrink and the war party to swell.

Thus when General James H. Carleton decided to end the Navajo scourge for all time, a mutual hatred, fueled by generations of bloodshed, plunder, and enslavement, fixed the setting within which each side regarded the other. To expect either to subordinate strategy or tactics to considerations of humanity ignores the grievances and passions of decades.

Kit Carson was General Carleton's willing tool — willing in two senses. First was merely the habit of subordination and obedience implicit in the military chain of command. Carson was a colonel following the orders of his superior, a brigadier general. In this instance, moreover, the superior was a haughty, imperious autocrat who demanded instant deference. Second was Carson's innate respect for authority figures — an understandable trait in an illiterate frontiersman moving in educated circles. As he had with John C. Frémont, Carson accorded Carleton (an old friend whom he had served a decade earlier) undeviating loyalty, admiration, and subordination that lent color to charges that he was a pliable tool of the military despot in Santa Fe.

The two proved a winning combination. Kit knew the country, the Indians, and the New Mexican volunteers who composed the military forces. He had shown an aptitude for military command that made him a moderately successful field officer. But it was Carleton's leadership that supplied the critical catalyst. His paternalistic manipulation — now prodding, now scolding, now lecturing, now praising — gave direction, energy, and success to efforts that could easily have foundered in confusion and lassitude. Carson alone did not conquer the Navajos in the winter of 1863–1864. The team of Carleton and Carson deserves the acclaim or the reproach, as the case may be.

The conquest of the Navajos occurred in three distinct stages, each of which merits its own judgment by history, and by its victims. These are Carson's military operations in the winter of 1863–1864, the "Long Walk" across New Mexico to the Pecos River in 1864, and the four-year confinement on the Bosque Redondo Reservation of 1864 to 1868. Kit Carson had little or nothing to do with the Long Walk or the Bosque Redondo experiment, although he certainly condoned the latter if not the former. He can fairly be held accountable only for the roundup that made these final two stages possible.

The Navajo Roundup was not Carson's idea, nor even Carleton's, for that matter. Carleton's predecessor, General Edward R. S. Canby, had concluded that the only enduring solution to the long-festering conflict with the Navajo was "their removal and colonization at points so remote from the settlements as to isolate them entirely from the inhabitants of the territory."[6] The outbreak of the Civil War had thwarted Canby's plans for rounding up the Navajo and confining them on a distant reservation. Carleton picked up where Canby had left off.

Central to the Canby strategy was recognizing no distinction between *ricos* and *ladrones*. The entire tribe would be held accountable for the actions of its members. As Carleton lectured one of his officers, "There is no peace party of Navajoes. . . . The whole tribe is a war party, and as such will be treated alike. . . . The rule is a plain one, and needs no further correspondence."[7]

The roundup directed by Kit Carson was a military operation conducted in time of war. For both sides, all enemies in their person and property were fair game — as they had been in Navajo hostilities since Spanish times. Carson's purpose, however, was less to kill Navajos than to impoverish them. Destroying their flocks, orchards, crops, food stores, dwellings, horses, and other possessions, he and Carleton expected, would destroy their will to resist. Mass surrenders would then set the stage for deportation to the remote reservation Canby had envisaged.

The Navajo Roundup anticipated the "total war" that Generals William T. Sherman and Philip H. Sheridan would inaugurate a year later against the Southern Confederacy. It rested on the same reasoning that explained Sherman's march from Atlanta to the sea and Sheridan's ravaging of the Shenandoah Valley. It was the total war, moreover, that these same generals waged against the Plains Indians in the years after the Civil War.

Total war fell on the total population. Men, women, and children suffered, and sometimes noncombatants died — from starvation and exposure, however, rather than from musket balls. All endured constant fear and insecurity that fed the impulse to give up. Extending war beyond the fighting man to his family was deliberate, rationalized with the notion that it ended the war more quickly and was therefore more humane.

Carson conducted the roundup on these principles. In five separate sweeps through the Navajo country, he seized their stock, destroyed their crops and orchards, and kept them constantly on the run and increasingly demoralized. Even more destructive were the forays of independent plundering parties over which he had no control: Utes; Pueblos from Zuni, Jemez, and the Hopi towns; and New Mexicans from the Rio Grande settlements. By the end of 1863, these incursions into the Navajo homeland had killed seventy-eight and wounded forty people — hardly a genocidal toll. But the devastation had been appalling and the psychological effect decisive. By March 1864, six thousand people, half the tribe, had surrendered; and by the end of the year more than eight thousand had been uprooted and set down on the arid wastelands of the Bosque Redondo.[8]

In purely military terms, both the plan and its execution were a resounding success. In humanitarian terms, especially in hindsight, the conquest of the Navajos leads to more ambiguous judgments.

My own judgment as a historian is this: Kit Carson's Navajo Roundup was no less humane than most wars at any time and place in history — certainly no less than many operations of the Civil War taking place at that very time in the East and South. The strategy was Carleton's, derived from Canby. Its purpose was to cause enough suffering to convince the Navajo people to give up and leave their homeland. Under Carson's direction, it succeeded in that purpose, although independent, nonmilitary raiding parties caused as much suffering as Carson's military sweeps. To convict Carson individually of inhumanity requires similar conviction of a host of other commanders throughout history, including those who ordered the bombing of Berlin and Tokyo in World War Two and Hanoi in the Vietnam War. War is not a humane activity.

Far more vulnerable to the charge of inhumanity, it seems to me, is General Carleton. In 1863's climate of malice, his strategy was not an unreasonable response to the challenge. As carried out by Carson, the Navajo Roundup exacted no greater human toll than necessary to carry out the strategy.

Then came the Long Walk and Bosque Redondo. Here was the inhumanity, and Carleton bears the most blame. The Long Walk did not require the suffering of the roundup. The people had surrendered. Carleton commanded the military resources to move the Navajos across the territory at far less cost in hunger, hardship, and exposure. Their misery owed less to military brutality than to administrative and logistical failings. And these failings, in turn, sprang less from incompetence or inefficiency than from the sudden and unexpected success of Carson's roundup; no one foresaw the surrender of half the Navajo tribe. As commanding general, however, Carleton bears the responsibility.

Carleton's biggest blunder was the Bosque Redondo. It could not sustain as many Indians in agricultural and pastoral self-subsistence as he moved there. Nor did the government prove capable of supporting the Navajo. Yet year after year Carleton refused to admit error and continued to worsen the tragedy, even as the evidence became overwhelming.

Even more tragic for the Navajo than hunger and disease was their despondency over separation from their homeland. With his literal mind and ignorance of other cultures, Carleton probably cannot be faulted for failing to understand the depth of the Navajos' attachment to their homeland. Any formula that severed their roots in the soil of their ancestors was doomed to fail and to inflict such emotional pain as to constitute inhumanity.

From today's perspective, with its sense of outrage over the victimization of the Indians, we try to search out the responsible villains. A test of fairness demands that we understand the milieu in which our forebears functioned and that we reproach them severely only when their actions violated the norms of their time and place. This admonition, it should be stressed, applies to judgments of Indians acting consistently with their culture as well as to whites acting in accord with theirs. Against this backdrop, it seems to me that Dear Old Kit is far less the scoundrel than James H. Carleton.

NOTES

1. W.W.H. Davis, *El Gringo, or New Mexico and Her People* (Santa Fe, N.M.: Rydal Press, 1938), p. 168.
2. Quoted in Thelma S. Guild and Harvey L. Carter, *Kit Carson: A Pattern for Heroes* (Lincoln: University of Nebraska Press, 1984), p. 210.
3. Carson to Cutler, January 4, 1863, C24/1863, RG 98, National Archives and Records Service.
4. Annual Reports of the Commissioner of Indian Affairs, 1857, p. 568; 1858, pp. 194–195; 1859, p. 343.
5. This relationship is a constant theme in the official military and civil correspondence of New Mexico during the 1850s. It emerges most clearly in the documents contained in Annie H. Abel, ed., *The Correspondence of James S. Calhoun* (Washington, D.C.: GPO, 1915); but see also testimony of various officials of long residence in Santa Fe taken there in 1865 and printed in *Condition of the Indian Tribes*, Senate Reports, 39th Cong., 2d sess., no. 156, pp. 325–37.
6. Canby to governor of New Mexico, November 22, 1861, encl. to Canby to Assistant Adjutant General Western Department, December 1, 1861, N315/1861, RG 94, National Archives and Records Service.
7. Carleton to Lt. Col. J. Francisco Chavez, August 7, 1863, *Condition of the Indian Tribes*, p. 126.
8. The movements, casualties, and population figures in this paragraph are drawn from voluminous official sources cited in my *Frontiersmen in Blue: The United States Army and the Indian, 1848–1865* (New York: Macmillan, 1963; Lincoln: University of Nebraska Press, 1981), pp. 237–247.

Contributors

R. C. Gordon-McCutchan received his Ph.D. from Princeton University. He teaches history and philosophy for the University of New Mexico–Taos and is director of the Kit Carson Historic Museums. He has written numerous articles in nineteenth-century American studies and is the author of the award-winning *The Taos Indians and the Battle for Blue Lake.*

Lawrence C. Kelly received his Ph.D. from the University of New Mexico and is a professor of history at the University of North Texas. He is the author of *The Navajo Indians and Federal Indian Policy, 1900–1935, The Navajo Roundup, The Assault on Assimilation,* and *Federal Indian Policy.*

Darlis A. Miller received her Ph.D. from the University of New Mexico and is a professor of history at New Mexico State University. She is the author of *The California Column in New Mexico, Soldiers and Settlers: Military Supply in the Southwest,* and *Captain Jack Crawford, A Genius in Buckskin.*

Marc S. Simmons received his Ph.D. from the University of New Mexico and is a professional historian and author of the Southwest. His writing, lectures, and research focus on the Indian and Hispanic heritages of New Mexico. He is the author of *Albuquerque, A Narrative History, Witchcraft in the Southwest,* and *Murder on the Santa Fe Trail* as well as numerous other books.

Robert M. Utley received his M.A. from Indiana University and served the National Park Service for twenty-five years in various capacities, including as chief historian. He is the author of a number of significant books, among them: *The Lance and the Shield, Billy the Kid,* and *Cavalier in Buckskin.*

Index

Adams, Robert, 2
"Adventure of Kit Carson, A Tale of the Sacramento, An," 5
Ahdilohee ("The Rope Thrower"), 45
Aiken, Albert W., *Kit Carson, King of Guides,* 7, 10
Albuquerque, A Narrative History (Simmons), 99
Albuquerque Public Library, 77
American Indian Movement, 88n20
American Indians. *See* Indians; *individual tribes*
Apaches, 7, 8, 15, 33, 74, 79, 80
Army and the Navajo (Thompson), 56–57, 69
Averill, Charles, *Kit Carson, Prince of the Gold Hunters,* 5, 83

Bailey, Lynn R., 26, 49, 57, 58, 69; *Indian Slave Trade in the Southwest,* 51; *The Long Walk,* 21, 49, 50–51
Barboncito, 34
Beadle, Erastus, 1–2
Beadle, Irwin, 2
Beadle, John Hanson, *The Undeveloped West, or Five Years in the Territories,* 54–55
Beadle & Adams, 1–2, 4, 6, 17n3
Beale, Edward F., 15, 16; "Kit Carson's Shade," 16
Begay, Dugal Tsosie, 81
Bennett, Emerson, *The Prairie Flower,* 5
Berkhofer, F., *The White Man's Indian,* 8
Bighorse, Tiana, *Bighorse the Warrior,* 87n5
Bilagaana, 36, 63
Billy the Kid, 22
Billy the Kid (Utley), 99
Black Hills gold rush, 4
Blackwelder, Bernice, *Great Westerner,* 49, 50
Blakeney, Major Thomas, 29, 38, 39, 40
Bonito River, 93
Booklist, 21
Boone, Daniel, xi, 3
Bosque Redondo, xi, 21, 28, 30, 33, 38, 40, 41, 43, 45, 51, 52, 53, 57, 63, 64, 77, 81, 94, 95, 96, 97
Boyle, Pat, 84
Buell, Crawford R., "The Navajo 'Long Walk,'" 54
Burdett, Charles, *Kit Carson: The Life and Adventures of Christopher Carson,* 6
Butler, Ann M., 86

California, 4, 26
California Column in New Mexico (Miller), 99
Campbell, George, 61, 66–67
Canby, General E.R.S., 25, 26, 27, 31, 57, 59, 65, 81, 95, 97; campaign of, 51, 53, 54, 63
Cañon Bonito, 51, 62
Canyon de Chelly, 32, 37, 40, 41–43, 51, 52, 56, 57, 61, 62, 68, 75
Canyon del Muerto, 56
Captain Jack Crawford, A Genius in Buckskin (Miller), 99
Carey, Captain Asa, 33, 67
Carleton, General James H., 21, 52, 54, 61, 62, 63–64, 66; and Carson, 31–33, 93, 94–95; and the Navajo War, 26–30, 40, 94, 97, 98
Carson campaign, xi, 51, 53, 55, 56, 65, 68, 74
Carson, Christopher Houston. *See* Carson, Kit
Carson, Josepha, 85
Carson, Juan, 83
Carson, Kit, 3; appearance of, ix, x; attitude toward Indians, 50, 77–84, 92–93; biographies of, 5–6, 16, 49, 50, 74, 78; and Carleton, 31–33, 93, 94–95; children of, 50, 83; correspondence of, 52; death of, xi, 15; and dime novels, 15, 83–84, 89n44; fictionalized accounts of, x; gravesite of, 85; as guide, x, 4, 92; independence of, 31–33; as Indian agent, 82, 92, 93; Indian fighter, x, 1, 22, 24, 92; Indian killer, xin1, 1, 22, 24; likened to Adolph Hitler, 85; as literary character, 6–7, 83; memoirs of, xi, 5, 15, 49–50, 80, 82; as mountain man, ixn5, 78, 79, 92; myth of, 83–87; "pseudo-companions," 84; release of Navajo captives, 52; as "reluctant campaigner," 28, 31, 52, 60; reputation of, 16, 49–50, 69, 83, 87n5; subordinates of, 29, 39, 52, 67; wives of, 10, 28, 50, 82, 85, 92
Carson, Lindsey, 78
Carson, Mary Ann, 78
Carson National Forest, 75
Carter, Harvey L., xii, 16, 29, 43, 74, 76, 84; *Dear Old Kit,* 49, 50, 82
Carter, Harvey L. and Thelma S. Guild, *Kit Carson,* xi, 68
Cavalier in Buckskin (Utley), 99
Cebolleta, 66
Censorship, 3
Chacon, Captain Rafael, 40

Changing Ways of Southwestern Indians, The (Schroeder), 53, 54
Chavez, Colonel Francisco, 34
Chavez, Manuel, 65, 66
Cheyenne tribe, 80–81, 83–84
Chivington, John M., 83–84
Chivington massacre. *See* Sand Creek Massacre
Church Rock, New Mexico, 74
Civil Rights Movement, 73
Civil War, 1, 2, 24, 25, 26, 54, 95, 96, 97
Cody, Buffalo Bill, 3, 16
Collins, James L., 89
Colorado College, 76
Colorado Springs Gazette Telegraph, 76
Colorado State Capitol Hall of Fame, 84
Colorado volunteers, raid against Navajos, 67
Columbus, Christopher, 76, 91
Comanches, 7, 10, 26, 82
Common-law wives, 50
Conditions of the Indian Tribes (U.S. Senate document), 50, 65, 70
Confederate invasion of New Mexico, 26, 54, 55, 65
Correll, J. Lee, *Through White Men's Eyes,* 57, 63
Crawford, Captain Jack, 3, 4
Crockett, Davy, xi, 3, 22
Crop destruction. *See* Scorched earth campaign
Cubero, 66
Cummings, Major Joseph, 60
Custer, George Armstrong, 16, 91
Cutler, Captain Benjamin C., 32, 61, 89n42

Daklugie, Asa, 79
Deadwood Dick, 13
Dear Old Kit: The Historical Christopher Carson (Carter), 49, 50
Delgadito, 34, 41
Denver Post, 76
Dime novels, 1–19, 83–84, 89n44
Diné, 24. *See also* Navajos
Dinetah, 45
Drannon, Captain William, 84
Drinnon, Richard, 73, 78, 88n24

Earp, Wyatt, 22
Ellis, Edward S.: *Seth Jones,* 2, 6; *The Fighting Trapper,* 8; *The Life and Times of Christopher Carson,* 6, 8
Enemy Navajos, 55, 58
Estergreen, M. Morgan, *Kit Carson,* 49, 50
Extermination, 38, 39, 40, 41, 42, 84

Farming by Indians, 28, 50, 64, 93–94
Federal Indian Policy (Kelly), 99
Fighting Trapper: or, Kit Carson to the Rescue, The (Ellis), 8
Formula writing, 2

Fort Canby, 29, 38, 40, 61, 62
Fort Defiance, 26, 29, 32, 54, 55, 64
Fort Fauntleroy, 63, 65
Fort Garland, Colorado, x, 82
Fort Hempstead, 78
Fort Lyon, Colorado, 89n42
Fort Sill, 11
Fort Sumner, 81
Fort Wingate, 40, 54
Franklin, Missouri, ix, 78
Frémont, Jesse Benton, xii, 4, 15
Frémont, John Charles, ix–x, 4, 79, 93, 95
Fur trade, ix, 78, 80

Gallina, 40
Gardner, Mark L., ix–xiii
Genocide, xi, 76, 77, 82, 85, 96
Gila River, 80
Glorieta Pass, 26
Gold rush: Black Hills, 4; of 1849, 55
Gordon-McCutchan, R.C., 57, 99; "Rope Thrower and the Navajo," 21–47; *The Taos Indians and the Battle for Blue Lake,* 99
Government documents, 50, 54
Graydon, Captain James "Paddy," 59
Great Westerner: The Story of Kit Carson (Blackwelder), 49, 50
Guild, Thelma, xi, 16, 29, 43, 68, 74
Gunfighter Nation (Slotkin), 13
Gunnison, Colorado, 76, 77

Harbaugh, Thomas C., *Kiowa Charley, The White Mustanger,* 6, 10–13
Harpers Ferry Center, 75
Harper's Weekly, 15
Heroes, xi, xiiin9, 3, 23, 25, 86
Herrera Grande, 33, 38
Hickok, Wild Bill, 3, 16
Hillerman, Tony, 75, 77
Hispanics, 24, 25, 27, 82; raids by Navajos, 81; raids on Navajos, 54; slave trade, 51, 67
Historian's craft, distortions of, 57–68
Historical reality, 16
Hitler, Adolf, 76, 85
Holden's Dollar Magazine, 5
Holy People of the First World, 64
Hopi tribe, 33, 41, 96
"Horse Race at Fort Fauntleroy: An Incident of the Navajo Wars" (Simmons), 65
Horses, 23, 79
Hunting by Indians, 30, 50

Indian Affairs for New Mexico, 34
Indian Claims Commission, 55, 57
Indian Court of Claims, 55
Indian Reservations, 93, 95, 96
Indian Slave Trade in the Southwest (Bailey), 51

Index

Indian Wars (Utley and Washburn), 39
Indians: and Carson, xi; Carson's attitude toward, 50, 77–84, 92–93; descriptions of, 9; hunting and farming by, 28, 30, 50, 64, 93–94; raiding and stealing by, 24, 25, 44, 74, 79, 87; and retaliation principle, 79–80, 82, 94; as savages, 23, 44; settlement of, 24, 25, 50; stereotype of, 1, 10, 58; subjugation of, 8; as wives of white men, 50, 79–80, 82. *See also* Long Walk; Navajo Roundup; Navajos; Navajo War; Slave trade
Inman, Henry, *The Old Santa Fe Trail*, 15
Iowa tribe, 78

Jackson, Andrew, 85
James, Jesse, 3, 13
Jaramillo, Josefa, 10
Jarra, 61
Jefferson, Thomas, 83
Jemez tribe, 96
Jicarilla Apaches, 27, 92
Johnson, Broderick H., *Navajo Stories of the Long Walk*, 55, 56
Johnson, Paul, 85
Jones, Daryl, 6, 11
Joseph, Chief, 92
Jung, Carl, 87

Kaywaykla, James, 79
Keenan, Gerald, 52
Kelly, Lawrence C., 30, 38, 40, 99; *Federal Indian Policy*, 99; "Historiography of the Navajo Roundup," 49–71; *Navajo Roundup*, 22, 49, 53, 58, 59, 60, 61, 62, 64, 65, 66, 67, 68, 69; *Navajo Roundup, The Assault on Assimilation*, 99; *The Navajo Indians and Federal Indian Policy, 1900–1935*, 99
Kiowa Charley, *The White Mustanger; or, Rocky Mountain Kit's Last Scalp Hunt* (Harbaugh), 6
Kiowas, 9, 11, 26, 82
Kit Carson: A Pattern for Heroes (Carter and Guild), xi, 68
Kit Carson: A Portrait in Courage (Estergreen), 49, 50
"Kit Carson: Indian Fighter or Indian Killer?" (symposium), xii, 75, 86
Kit Carson, King of Guides (Aiken), 7
Kit Carson, Prince of the Gold Hunters (Averill), 5, 83
Kit Carson: The Life and Adventures of Christopher Carson, The Celebrated Rocky Mountain Hunter, Trapper, and Guide (Burdett), 6
Kit Carson (steamboat), xiiin4
Kit Carson Campaign: The Last Great War Navajo War, The (Trafzer), 57–68
Kit Carson Cave, 74
Kit Carson Days, 1809–1868: Adventures in the Path of Empire (Sabin), 49, 50, 51

Kit Carson Historic Museums, xii, 99
Kit Carson Home, xi
Kit Carson's Autobiography (Quaife, editor), 49, 50
Kit Carson's Boys; or, With the Great Scout on His Last Trail (Old Scout), 10, 13–14
"Kit Carson's Ride" (Miller), 15, 16
"Kit Carson's Shade" (Beale), 16
Kit Carson State Park, 75
Kurtz, Josh, 90

Ladrones, 94, 95
Lakota people, 92
Lance and the Shield, The (Utley), 99
Largo, Jose, 59
Lewis, Harriet, 6
Lewis, Julius Warren ("Leon"), *Red Knife*, 6
Library of Congress, 50, 51, 52
Life and Adventures of Kit Carson, the Nestor of the Rocky Mountains, The (Peters), 5
Life and Times of Christopher Carson: The Rocky Mountain Scout and Guide, The (Ellis), 6
Limerick, Patricia Nelson, 71n25, 86, 88n18
Lipps, Oscar, 45
Little Colorado River, 33
Little Foot, 40
"Long March, 1863–1867, The" (McNitt), 53
Long Walk, 30, 43, 45, 51, 52–53, 75, 77, 95, 97; and food poisoning, 68; killing of captives, 51, 52, 55, 56; oral histories of, 54, 55–56
Long Walk: A History of the Navajo Wars, 1846–1868, The (Bailey), 21, 49, 50–51

McNitt, Frank: *Navajo Wars*, 53, 59, 63, 65, 69; "The Long March, 1863–1867," 53, 55
Malaeska; The Indian Wife of the White Hunter (Stephens), 2
Manifest destiny doctrine, 93
Manuelito, 33, 38–39, 59, 81
"Massacre" at Fort Fauntleroy, 65–66
Maxwell, Lucien, 5
Memoirs of Carson, xi, 5, 15, 49–50, 80, 82
Mescalero Apaches, 26, 28, 82, 93
Mexican-American War, x
Military policy, 25–26
Miller, Darlis A., 1–19, 49, 99; *Captain Jack Crawford, A Genius in Buckskin*, 99; "Kit Carson and Dime Novels: The Making of a Legend," 1–19; *The California Column in New Mexico*, 99; *Soldiers and Settlers: Military Supply in the Southwest*, 99
Miller, Joaquin, "Kit Carson's Ride," 15, 16
Missouri River steamboat, ix, x
Mitchell, Frank, 87
Montoya, Lieutenant Donacio, 59
Murder on the Santa Fe Trail (Simmons), 99
My Lai massacre, 87

Myth of Kit Carson, 83–87

Nahondzod (the fearing time), 53
National Archives, 50–51, 52
National Park Service, 75, 99
Native Americans. *See* Indians; *individual tribes*
Navaho Indians and Federal Indian Policy, 1900–1935, The (Kelly), 99
Navajo Community College, 88n14
"Navajo 'Long Walk'; Recollections by Navajos, The" (Buell), 54
Navajo Roundup: Selected Correspondence of Kit Carson's Expedition Against the Navajo, 1863–1865 (Kelly), 22, 49, 53, 58, 59, 60, 61, 62, 64, 65, 66, 67, 68, 69
Navajo Roundup, 49–71, 95–97. *See also* Navajo War
Navajo Roundup, The Assault on Assimilation (Kelly), 99
Navajos, 82; archival documents of, 57; as captives, 52; crop destruction (*see* Scorched earth campaign); culture of, 24–25, 43–45, 97, 98; elders, 45; food poisoning, 67–68; "hostiles and friendlies," 34–34; livestock slaughters, 51, 53, 54, 55, 56; oral histories of, 43, 54, 55–56, 57, 68, 75; political organization of, 94; as portrayed by Trafzer, 22–23; raiding and stealing, 24, 25, 44, 74, 81–82, 87, 94; raids by Hispanics and Indians, 54, 74; rape by soldiers, 55, 56; religious beliefs, 64; relocation of, 27, 28, 29, 39, 54, 57; sacred homeland, 23, 64, 97; and Spanish contact, 53; starvation of, 30, 33–34, 43, 54, 64, 65, 75; surrender by, 29, 30, 33, 35, 36, 37, 38, 40, 42, 52, 54, 67, 96, 97; women and children, 36–37. *See also* Indians; Long Walk; Navaho Roundup; Navajo War
Navajo Stories of the Long Walk (Johnson), 55, 56
Navajo Tribal Land Claims Office, 51
Navajo War, 23–24, 26–30, 45, 53, 54, 57, 94. *See also* Navajo Roundup
Navajo Wars: Military Campaigns, Slave Raids, and Reprisals (McNitt), 53, 59, 65, 69
Navajo Yearbook, 1951–1961, 55
New Mexico, 26, 27, 54, 55, 65
New Mexico Endowment for the Humanities, xii
New Mexico Indian Superintendency Records, 59
New western historians, xii, 86, 88
New York Times, xii
New York Tribune, 3
Nez Perce tribe, 92
Nichols, John, 76, 77

Ohio University, xi
Old Santa Fe Trail, The (Inman), 15
Oral histories, 43, 54, 55–56, 57, 68, 75
Oregon, 4
Original documents, 58

Paiute tribe, 65
Papagos tribe, 80
Pawnee tribe, 4
Peach orchards destroyed, 51, 68
Pecos River, 81, 93, 95
Peters, DeWitt C., *The Life and Adventures of Kit Carson, the Nestor of the Rocky Mountains*, 5
Pfeiffer, Captain, 62, 68
Plains Indians, 24, 79, 96
Plympton, Captain P.W.S., 33
Postle, Lieutenant, 61
Prairie Flower, The (Bennett), 5
Presentism, 22–23, 91–92
Pruett Press, 52
Public opinion, 85, 86
Pueblo, Colorado, 32, 61
Pueblo Indians, 23, 24, 25, 27, 74, 81, 96

Quaife, Milo M., editor, *Kit Carson's Autobiography*, 49, 50

Racism, 78, 82, 85, 88
Rape of Navajo women, 55, 56
Rayado, New Mexico, 81
Red Clothes campaign, 38
Redford, Robert, 77
Red Knife; or, Kit Carson's Last Trail (Lewis), 6
Reputation of Carson, 49–50, 69
Research methods of Clifford Trafzer, 57–58
Retaliation principle, 79–80, 82, 94
Revenge. *See* Retaliation principle
Revisionist historians, xii, 58, 71
Rhetoric of Clifford Trafzer, 22–23
Richardson, Albert, 86–87
Ricos, 94, 95
Rio Grande, 26, 95, 96
Rio Pecos, 21
Rocky Mountains, ix, 4
Roessel, Ruth, 56
Rusling, General James F., 82
Rutledge, Colonel Dick, 84

Sabin, Edwin L., *Kit Carson Days, 1809–1868: Adventures in the Path of Empire*, 49, 50, 51
Sac tribe, 78
Sacramento Valley, 78
Sagel, Jim, 75
Salt River, 80
San Joaquin Valley, 78
Sand Creek Massacre, 37, 83
Sandoval, 58
Sangre de Cristo Range, 75
Santa Fe Historical Society, 54
Santa Fe National Historic Trail, 75
Santa Fe Reporter, xii, 71n25
Santa Fe Trail caravan, ix, 80–81
Sarracino, Pedro, 40
Savages, 23, 44

Index

Schroeder, Albert H., *The Changing Ways of Southwestern Indians*, 53, 54
Scorched earth campaign, 29–30, 33–34, 35, 42, 51, 52, 53, 54, 56, 57, 58, 59, 64, 75, 96, 97
Scripps Howard News Service, xi
"Second Battle for the West, The," xii, 71
Sena, Major, 62
Seth Jones; or, The Captives of the Frontier (Ellis), 2, 6
Settlers, 25, 26, 27
Sheep reduction program of 1930s, 56
Sheep slaughter. *See* Navajos, livestock slaughters
Sheridan, Philip H., 96
Sherman, William T., 15, 96
Sign language, 80, 92
Silver Bell, 10
Simmons, Marc S., 44, 99; *Albuquerque, A Narrative History*, 99; "Horse Race at Fort Fauntleroy: An Incident of the Navajo Wars," 65; "Kit and the Indians," 73–90; *Murder on the Santa Fe Trail*, 99; *Witchcraft in the Southwest*, 99
Sioux, 4, 11, 13
Slave trade, 51, 58, 60, 66–67
Slotkin, Richard, *Gunfighter Nation*, 13
Smith, Henry Nash, 2, 6
Society for the Betterment of the Red Man, 84–85
Soldiers, 39, 92
Soldiers and Settlers: Military Supply in the Southwest (Miller), 99
Sordo, 40
Spanish and Navajo contact, 53
Spanish language, 83, 92
Starvation. *See* Navajos, starvation of
Steam-rotary press, 2, 17n3
Steck, Michael, 34
Steckmesser, Kent, 6
Stephens, Ann S., *Malaeska*, 2
Symposium on Carson, xii, xivn13, 75, 86

Taos, New Mexico, xi, 28
Taos Indians and the Battle for Blue Lake, The (Gordon-McCutchan), 99
Taos News, xii, 75
Thomas, General Lorenzo, 62, 64
Thompson, Captain John, 68
Thompson, Gerald, *The Army and the Navajo*, 56–57, 69
Through White Men's Eyes (Correll), 57, 63
Tousey, Frank, 3
Traditional scholars, xii, 86
Trafzer, Clifford, 30–43, 49, 69; biases of, 22–23; interpretation of sources, 69; *The Kit Carson Campaign: The Last Great War Navajo War*, 21–23, 57–68; research methods, 57–58

Trappers, ix, 78, 79, 92
Treaties, 23, 25, 26, 27, 63
Underhill, Ruth M., 74
Undeveloped West, or Five Years in the Territories, The (Beadle), 54–55
U.S. Congress, 4
U.S. Corps of Topographical Engineers, 4
U.S. Indian policy, 93
U.S. military policy, 25–26
Ute Indians, 24, 25, 55, 56, 60, 64, 66, 74, 81, 92, 93, 94, 96
Utley, Robert M., 99; "An Indian Before Breakfast: Kit Carson Then and Now," 91–98; *Billy the Kid*, 99; *Cavalier in Buckskin*, 99; *The Lance and the Shield*, 99
Utley, Robert M. and Wilcomb E. Washburn, *Indian Wars*, 39

Vandalism, 84–85
Velasques, Chico, 8
Victor, Orville, 3
Vietnam War, 73, 97
Villains, 86, 98
Volunteer raids, 67

Wagon trains, 23, 80–81
Walker, John R., 80
Walters, Harry, 88n14
War of the Rebellion, The, 50, 69
Washington Chronicle, x
Washington Union, 83
West, ix, x, 3; mythic, 16, 17
Western films, 25
Whiskey, 82
White man, 24; culture of, 98; expansion of, 16, 43, 93; and Indian relocation, 24, 25, 50; and Navajo archival documents, 57; racism of, 78; and retaliation principle, 79–80, 82, 94; and women, 9
White Man's Indian, The (Berkhofer), 8
White, Mrs. James M., 15
Wiggins, Oliver Perry, 84
Winter campaign, 32, 52, 65, 95
Winthrop, Josiah, S., 84–85
Witchcraft in the Southwest (Simmons), 99
Witt, Shirley Hill, 76, 77
Women, in dime novels, 9–10
Wootton, "Uncle Dick," 79
Workman, David, ix
World War Two, 97
Wounded Knee, 92

Young, Ewing, 78–79, 80

Zuni tribe, 96